Outdoor Woodworking Projects

Complete Handyman's Library™
Handyman Club of America
Minneapolis, Minnesota

Published in 1996 by
Handyman Club of America
12301 Whitewater Drive
Minnetonka, Minnesota 55343

Published by arrangement with Creative Publishing international, Inc.
ISBN 0-86573-662-6

Printed on American paper by
R. R. Donnelley & Sons Co.
02 01 00 99 98 / 5 4 3 2 1

CREDITS:
Created by: The Editors of Creative Publishing international, Inc. and the staff of the Handyman Club of America in cooperation with Black & Decker. **BLACK&DECKER** is a trademark of Black & Decker (US), Incorporated and is used under license.

Handyman Club of America:
    Vice President, Product Marketing: Mike Vail
    Book Marketing Director: Cal Franklin
    Book Products Development Manager: Steve Perlstein
    Book Marketing Coordinator: Jay McNaughton

Contents

Introduction

Outdoor living is becoming the country's favorite pastime. The information in this book will show you how to build a wide array of clever projects that will enhance your enjoyment of your yard, garden, deck porch and patio. Whether you enjoy simple relaxation time on your deck or patio, or you prefer down-and-dirty work in the garden, you need inexpensive, yet visually pleasing, furnishings to get the most out of your valuable time.

In *Outdoor Woodworking Projects* you'll find complete plans and instructions for 35 functional, attractive outdoor furnishings.

From a simple cedar patio table to an elaborate garden bridge, the projects in this book have two things in common: they make outdoor living more enjoyable; and they can be built easily, cheaply and without the need for a workshop full of fancy tools.

Outdoor Woodworking Projects is a book of plans. In it you'll find detailed information in the form of step-by-step instructions, full-color photographs, complete cutting and shopping lists and precise construction drawings for all 35 outdoor building projects. Every project in this book can be built using only basic hand tools and portable power tools that you probably already own. And you won't need to spend hours scouring specialty woodworking stores for the materials and hardware you'll need. We used only products that are sold in most building centers and corner hardware stores to make these items.

Among the many clever projects in this book, you'll find: a picnic table built for two; an Oriental-style freestanding arbor; a versatile Adirondack chair; two styles of cedar planters; a spacious garden cart made from cedar; a grill garage that's designed to hold newer-style gas grills; and many more useful backyard items you may never have thought you could build yourself.

Organizing Your Worksite

Portable power tools and hand tools offer a level of convenience that is a great advantage over stationary power tools. But using them safely and conveniently requires some basic housekeeping. Whether you are working in a garage, a basement or outdoors, it is important that you establish a flat, dry holding area where you can store tools. Set aside a piece of plywood on sawhorses, or dedicate an area of your workbench for tool storage, and be sure to return tools to that area once you are finished with them. It is also important that all waste, including lumber scraps and sawdust, be disposed of in a timely fashion. Check with your local waste disposal department before throwing away any large scraps of building materials or any finishing-material containers.

Safety Tips
•*Always wear eye and hearing protection when operating power tools and performing any other dangerous activities.*
•*Choose a well-ventilated work area when cutting or shaping wood and when using finishing products.*

Tools & Materials

At the start of each project, you will find a set of symbols that show which power tools are used to complete the project as it is shown (see below). You will also need a set of basic hand tools: a hammer, screwdrivers, tape measure, a level, a combination square, C-clamps, and pipe or bar clamps. You will also find a shopping list of all the construction materials you will need. Miscellaneous materials and hardware are listed with the cutting list that accompanies the construction drawing. When buying lumber, note that the "nominal" size of the lumber is usually larger than the "actual size." For example, a 2×4 is actually $1\frac{1}{4} \times 3\frac{1}{8}$"

Power Tools You Will Use

Circular saw to make straight cuts. For long cuts and rip-cuts, use a straightedge guide. Install a carbide-tipped combination blade for most projects.

Drills: use a cordless drill for drilling pilot holes and counterbores, and to drive screws; use an electric drill for sanding and grinding tasks.

Jig saw for making contoured cuts and internal cuts. Use a combination wood blade for most projects where you will cut pine, cedar or plywood.

Power sander to prepare wood for a finish and to smooth out sharp edges. Owning several power sanders (⅓-sheet, ¼-sheet, and belt) is helpful.

Belt Sander For resurfacing rough wood. Can also be used as a stationary sander when mounted on its side on a flat worksurface.

Router to cut decorative edges and roundovers in wood. As you gain more experience, use routers for cutting grooves (like dadoes) to form joints.

Guide to Building Materials Used in this Book

•Sheet goods:
PLYWOOD: Basic good sold in several grades (from CDX to AB) and thicknesses. BCX is well-suited for outdoor projects.
CEDAR PLYWOOD: Plywood with a rough-sawn cedar face.
TILEBOARD: Thin hardboard with a hard moisture-resistant face.
CEMENTBOARD: Heavy cement-based panels sold in $3 \times 5'$ sheets.
HOUSE SIDING: Cedar or fir based exterior plywood, usually with vertical grooves 4" or 8" on-center. Most is ⅝" thick.
LATTICE PANELS: Lattice sheets from ½" to 1" thick, made from cedar or pressure-treated pine.

•Dimension lumber:
PINE: A basic, versatile softwood. "Select" and "#2 or better" are suitable grades. Requires a water-resistant finish.
PRESSURE-TREATED PINE: Pine boards impregnated with chemicals to resist rot. Green and brown treated are most common.
CEDAR: Excellent outdoor lumber with rich warm color. Usually sanded on one side and rough-textured on the other.
CEDAR SIDING: Beveled lap siding for cladding projects.

Guide to Fasteners & Adhesives Used in this Book

•Fasteners & Hardware:
WOOD SCREWS: Brass or steel; most projects use screws with a #6 or #8 shank. Can be driven with a power driver.
DECK SCREWS: Galvanized for weather resistance. Widely spaced threads for good gripping power in soft lumber.
NAILS & BRADS: Choose galvanized or brass.
CARRIAGE BOLTS: Like lag bolts, but with round heads: ⅜ to ⅝".
LAG SCREWS: Heavy-duty fasteners for extra holding strength.
MISCELLANEOUS HARDWARE: Use galvanized, brass, or plastic hinges, door pulls, and specialty hardware as required.

•Adhesives:
MOISTURE-RESISTANT WOOD GLUE: Any exterior wood glue, such as plastic resin glue
TILEBOARD & CONSTRUCTION ADHESIVE: Sold in cartridges and applied with a caulk gun to bond sheet goods.

•Miscellaneous materials:
Wood plugs (for filling screw counterbores); 1" 22-gauge copper strips; galvanized metal flashing; ceramic or stone floor tile; 3×8 concrete pavers; plexiglas; others as required.

Finishing Your Project

Sand all surfaces to remove rough spots and splinters, using medium-grit (120 to 150) sandpaper. Insert wood plugs into screw counterbores and sand until smooth. Fine finishsanding is usually not necessary for unpainted exterior projects, built cover nail and screw heads with wood putty, then sand with 180-grit sandpaper if you are painting. Most projects in this book are finished with exterior wood stain or clear wood sealer. Look for products that block UV rays, and follow the manufacturer's directions for application. When painting, use exterior primer, then apply enamel or glossy exterior paint

Patio Table

*This patio table blends sturdy construction with rugged style
to offer many years of steady service.*

CONSTRUCTION MATERIALS

Quantity	Lumber
2	4 × 4" × 10' cedar
2	2 × 2" × 10' cedar
2	1 × 4" × 8' cedar
3	1 × 6" × 8' cedar

Everyone knows a shaky, unstable patio table is a real headache, but you needn't be concerned about wobbly legs with this patio table. It is designed for sturdiness, with a close eye kept on style. As a result, this table will be a welcome addition to any backyard patio or deck.

This all-cedar patio table is roomy enough to seat six, and strong enough to support a large patio umbrella—even in high wind. The legs and cross-braces are cut from solid 4 × 4 cedar posts, then lag-bolted together. If you can find it at your local building center, buy heartwood cedar posts. Heartwood, cut from the center of the tree, is valued for its density, straightness, and resistance to decay. Because it is an eating surface, we applied a natural, clear linseed-oil finish.

OVERALL SIZE:
28" HIGH
40" WIDE
48" LONG

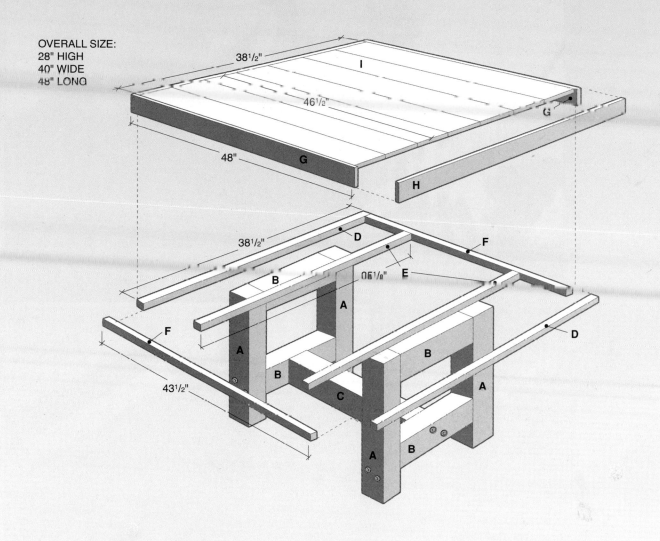

Cutting List						Cutting List				
Key	Part	Dimension	Pcs.	Material		Key	Part	Dimension	Pcs.	Material
A	Leg	3½ × 3½ × 27¼"	4	Cedar		F	Side cleat	1½ × 1½ × 43½"	2	Cedar
B	Stretcher	3½ × 3½ × 20"	4	Cedar		G	Side rail	¾ × 3½ × 48"	2	Cedar
C	Spreader	3½ × 3½ × 28"	1	Cedar		H	End rail	¾ × 3½ × 38½"	2	Cedar
D	End cleat	1½ × 1½ × 38½"	2	Cedar		I	Top slat	¾ × 5½ × 46½"	7	Cedar
E	Cross cleat	1½ × 1½ × 35½"	2	Cedar						

Materials: Moisture-resistant glue, deck screws (2", 2½"), (12) ⅜ × 6" lag bolts with washers, finishing materials.

Note: Measurements reflect the actual size of dimensional lumber.

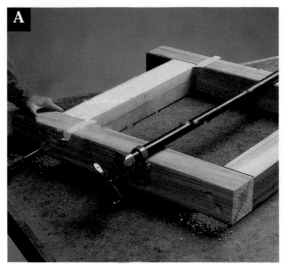

Counterbore two sets of holes on each leg to recess the lag bolts when you attach the legs to the stretchers.

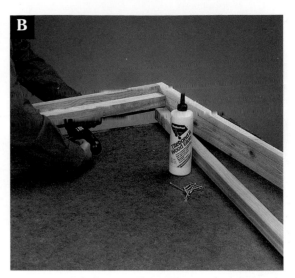

Maintain a ¾" distance from the top edge of the rails to the top edge of the cleats.

Directions: Patio Table

PREPARE THE LEG ASSEMBLY. Start by cutting the legs (A), stretchers (B) and spreader (C) to size from 4 × 4 cedar. Measure and mark 4" up from the bottom edge of each leg. These points mark the positions of the bottom edges of the lower stretchers. Test-fit the legs and stretchers to make sure they are square. The top stretchers should be flush against the top leg edges. Carefully position the pieces and clamp them together with pipe clamps. The metal jaws on the pipe clamps can damage the wood, so use protective clamping pads.

BUILD THE LEG ASSEMBLY. To complete this step, simply attach the legs to the stretchers, then connect the spreader to the stretchers. Start by drilling ⅞ × ⅜"-deep counterbored holes centered diagonally across the top end of each leg and opposite the lower stretchers **(photo A).** Drill ¼"-dia. pilot holes through each counterbored hole into the stretchers. Unclamp the pieces and drill ⅜"-dia. holes for lag bolts through the legs, using the pilot holes for center marks. Apply moisture-resistant glue to the ends of the stretchers, and attach the legs to the stretchers by driving ⅜ × 6" galvanized lag bolts with washers through the legs into the stretchers. Attach the spreader to the stretchers in the same way.

ATTACH THE CLEATS AND RAILS. Cut the side rails (G) and end rails (H) to size from 1 × 4 cedar. Drill two evenly spaced pilot holes for countersunk 2" deck screws through the ends of the side rails. Apply glue and

(below photo C)

Use pencils or dowels to set even gaps between top slats. Tape slats in position with masking tape.

Fasten cross cleats to the tabletop for strength, and to provide an anchor for the leg assembly.

Keep a firm grip on the tabletop slats when drilling deck screws through the cleats.

Before you stain or treat the patio table, sand the surfaces smooth.

fasten the side rails to the end rails with the screws. Cut the end cleats (D), cross cleats (E) and side cleats (F) from 2 × 2 cedar. Fasten the end cleats to the end rails ¾" below the top edges of the rails with glue and 2" deck screws **(photo B).** Repeat this procedure with the side cleats and side rails.

CUT & ATTACH THE TOP SLATS. Cut the top slats (I) to size from 1 × 6 cedar. Lay the slats into the tabletop frame so they rest on the cleats. Carefully spread the slats apart so they are evenly spaced. Use masking tape to hold the slats in place once you achieve the correct spacing **(photo C).** Stand the tabletop frame on one end, and fasten the top slats in place by driving 2" deck screws up through the end cleats into the slats, one at a time **(photo D).** Make sure you hold or clamp each slat firmly while fastening, or the screws will push the slats away from the frame.

CONNECT THE LEGS AND TOP. To complete the assembly of this project, turn the tabletop over and center the legs on the underside. Make sure that the legs are the same distance apart at the tabletop as they are at the bottom. Lay the cross cleats across the inside of the table legs. Use 2½" deck screws to fasten the cross cleats to the tabletop **(photo E),** then use 3" deck screws to fasten the cross cleats to the legs.

FINISH THE PATIO TABLE. For a more finished appearance, fill the exposed screw holes with cedar plugs or buttons (see TIP, previous page), and smooth the edges of the table and legs with a sander or router. If you want to fit the table with a patio umbrella, simply use a 1½"-dia. hole saw to cut a hole into the center of the tabletop. Use a drill and spade bit to cut the 1½"-diameter hole through the spreader. Sand the patio table to finished smoothness **(photo F).** Finish the table as desired—we used clear linseed oil for a natural, protective finish that is non-toxic.

Garden Bench

Graceful lines and trestle construction make this bench a charming complement to porches, patios and decks—as well as gardens.

CONSTRUCTION MATERIALS

Quantity	Lumber
1	2 × 8" × 6' cedar
4	2 × 2" × 10' cedar
1	2 × 4" × 6' cedar
1	2 × 6" × 10' cedar
1	2 × 2" × 6' cedar
1	1 × 4" × 12' cedar

Casual seating is a welcome addition to any outdoor setting. This lovely garden bench tucks neatly around the borders of any porch, patio or deck to create a pleasant resting spot for as many as three adults, without taking up a lot of space. Or, station this garden bench near your rear entry to use as convenient seating for removing shoes or setting down grocery bags while you unlock the door.

The straightforward design of this bench lends itself to accessorizing. Station a rustic cedar planter next to the bench for a lovely effect. Or add a framed lattice trellis to one side to cut down on wind and direct sun.

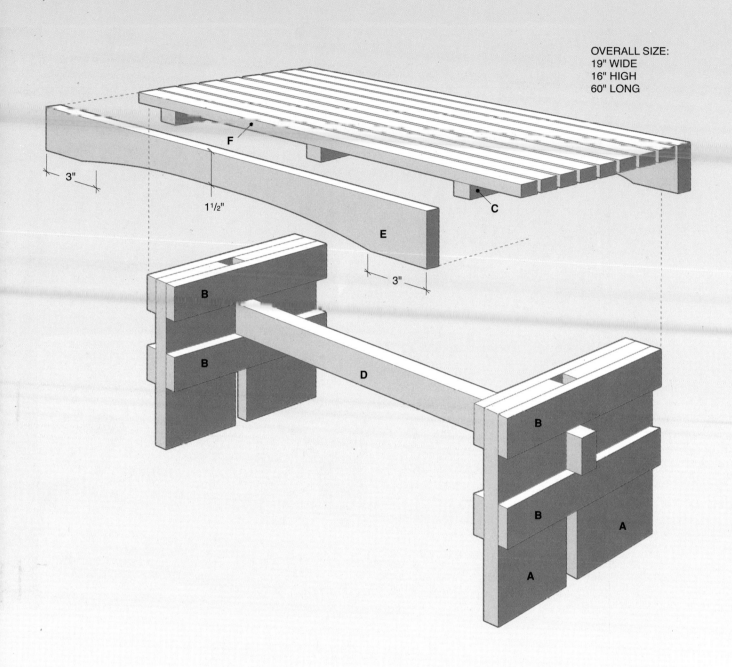

3"

1¹/₂"

F

C

3"

E

B

B

D

B

A

B

A

A

Cutting List

Key	Part	Dimension	Pcs.	Material
A	Leg half	1½ × 7¼ × 14½"	4	Cedar
B	Cleat	¾ × 3½ × 16"	8	Cedar
C	Brace	1½ × 1½ × 16"	3	Cedar
D	Trestle	1½ × 3½ × 60"	1	Cedar
E	Apron	1½ × 5½ × 60"	2	Cedar
F	Slat	1½ × 1½ × 60"	8	Cedar

Materials: Wood glue, wood sealer or stain, 3" wood screws, deck screws (1¼", 2").

Note: Measurements reflect the actual size of dimensional lumber.

11

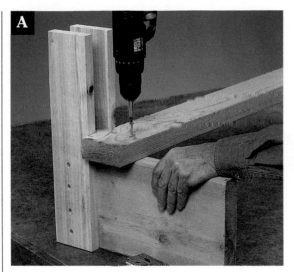

Make sure the stretcher is positioned correctly against the cleats, and attach it to the leg.

Attach the remaining leg half to the cleats on both ends to complete the leg assembly.

Directions: Arbor Bench

BUILD THE BASE. The base for this bench is composed of two sets of leg pairs connected by a full-length 2 × 4 trestle. Cut the leg halves (A), cleats (B) and trestle (D) to size. Start the assembly process by sandwiching one leg half between two cleats so the cleats are flush with the top and the outside edge of the leg half. Join the parts by driving four 1½" deck screws through each cleat and into the leg half, then assemble two more cleats with a leg half in the same fashion. Stand the two assemblies on end, with the open ends of the cleats pointing upward. Arrange the assemblies so they are roughly 4' apart, then set the trestle onto the inner edges of the leg halves, pressed flush against the bottoms of the cleats. Adjust the position of the assemblies so the trestle overhangs the leg half by 1½" at each end.

Attach the outer brace for the seat slats directly to the inside faces of the cleats.

Fasten the trestle to each leg half with glue and 2½" deck screws **(photo A)**. Attach another pair of cleats to each leg half directly below the first pair, positioned so each cleat is snug against the bottom of the trestle. Now, slide the other leg half between the cleats, keeping the top edge flush with the upper cleats. Join the leg halves with the cleats using glue and 2½" deck screws **(photo B)**. Cut the braces (C) from 2 × 2 cedar, then fasten

one brace to the inner top cleat on each leg assembly, so all tops are flush **(photo C)**.

MAKE THE APRONS. The graceful arch cut into each apron gives the bench some character. Begin to make the seat frame by cutting the aprons to size from 2 × 6 cedar. Lay out the arch onto one apron, starting 3" from each end. The peak of the arch, located over the midpoint of the apron, should be 1½" up from the bottom edge. To draw a smooth, even arch onto the apron, drive a casing nail at the peak of the arch, then drive nails at the starting points of the arch. Slip a flexible ruler behind the nails at the starting points and in front of the nail at the peak to create a smooth arch. Trace along the inside of the ruler to make a cutting line **(photo D).** Cut along the cutting line with a jig saw, then smooth out the cut with a sander. Trace the profile of the arch onto the other apron, then make and sand the cut. Once both aprons are sanded smooth, cut the slats to length from cedar 2 × 2s. Attach one slat to the top, inside edge of each apron with glue and deck screws **(photo E).**

INSTALL THE SEAT SLATS. Fasten the third brace (C) between the aprons, centered end to end on the project. Make sure the top of the brace is flush with the tops of the aprons. Position the six remaining slats on the braces so the gaps between slats are even (½"-thick spacers help maintain the even gaps). Attach the slat

with glue and 2½" deck screws driven up through the braces and into each slat **(photo F).**

APPLY THE FINISHING TOUCHES. Sand the seat slats with progressively finer sandpaper (start with 100-grit, sand up to 150-grit) to create a nice, smooth surface that is free of splinters. Wipe away the sanding residue with a rag dipped in mineral spirits. Let the bench dry completely, then apply whichever finish you choose. We used clear wood sealer to protect the cedar in our bench without altering the color. You

may prefer to use a wood stain first, but a protective coating is a good idea for any wood project that will be exposed to the elements.

Use a flexible ruler pinned between casing nails to trace a smooth arch onto the aprons.

Attach a 2 × 2 slat to the top, inside edge of each apron, using 2½" deck screws and glue.

Attach the seat slats with glue and 2½" deck screws. Insert ½"-thick spacers to set gaps between the slats.

Trellis Seat

Spice up your patio or deck with this sheltered seating structure. Set it in a secluded corner to create a warm, inviting outdoor living space.

CONSTRUCTION MATERIALS

Quantity	Lumber
1	4 × 4" × 6' cedar
2	2 × 8" × 8' cedar
4	2 × 4" × 12' cedar
1	1 × 6" × 10' cedar
8	1 × 2" × 8' cedar
2	½" × 4 × 4' cedar lattice

Made of lattice and cedar boards, our trellis seat is ideal for quiet moments of reading or conversing. The lattice creates just the right amount of privacy for a small garden or patio. It's an unobtrusive structure that is sure to add some warmth to your patio or deck. Position some outdoor plants along the top cap or around the frame sides to dress up the project and bring nature a little closer to home. For a cleaner appearance, conceal visible screw heads on the seat by counterboring the pilot holes for the screws and inserting cedar plugs (available at most woodworking stores) into the counterbores.

OVERALL SIZE:
51¾" HIGH
56½" WIDE
56½" LONG

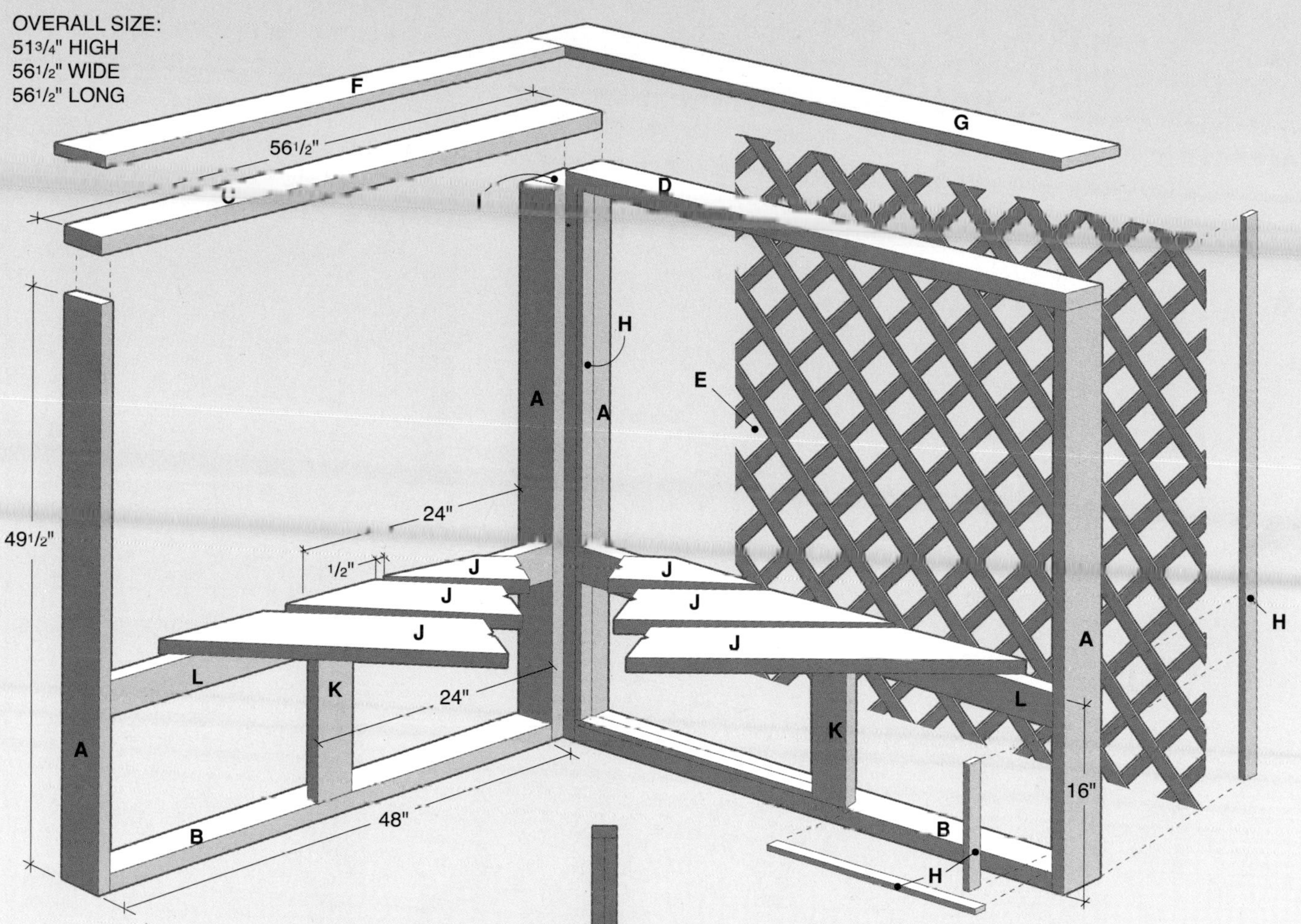

F
G
56½"
C
D
I
H
E
A
A
A
24"
½"
J
J
J
J
J
J
49½"
L
K
24"
A
K
L
H
16"
B
48"
B
H

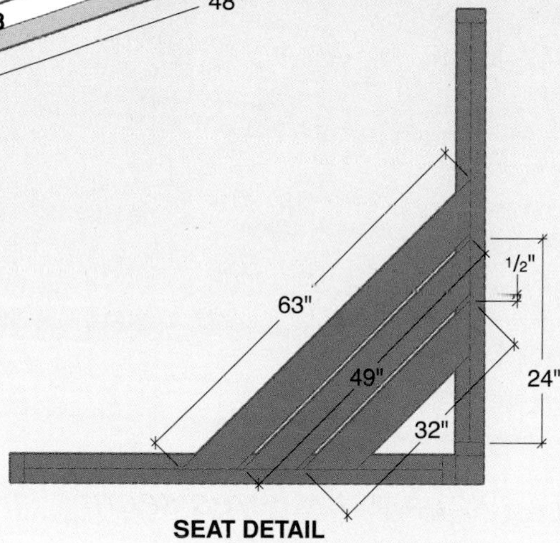

½"
63"
49"
24"
32"

SEAT DETAIL

Cutting List

Key	Part	Dimension	Pcs.	Material
A	Frame side	1½ × 3½ × 49½"	4	Cedar
B	Frame bottom	1½ × 3½ × 48"	2	Cedar
C	Long rail	1½ × 3½ × 56½"	1	Cedar
D	Short rail	1½ × 3½ × 51"	1	Cedar
E	Lattice	½ × 4 × 4'	2	Cedar
F	Short cap	¾ × 5½ × 51"	1	Cedar

Cutting List

Key	Part	Dimension	Pcs.	Material
G	Long cap	¾ × 5½ × 56½"	1	Cedar
H	Retaining strip	¾ × 1½" cut to fit	20	Cedar
I	Post	3½ × 3½ × 49½"	1	Cedar
J	Seat board	1½ × 7¼ × *	3	Cedar
K	Brace	1½ × 3½ × 11"	2	Cedar
L	Seat support	1½ × 3½ × 48"	2	Cedar

Materials: Moisture-resistant glue, deck screws (1¼", 2", 2½", 3"), finishing materials.

Note: Measurements reflect the actual size of dimensional lumber.

*Cut one each: 32", 49", 63"

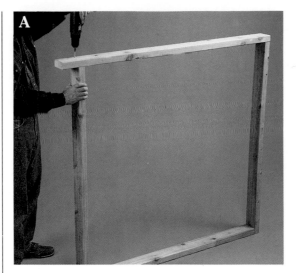

Attach the long rail at the top of one trellis frame with a 3½" overhang at one end to cover the post.

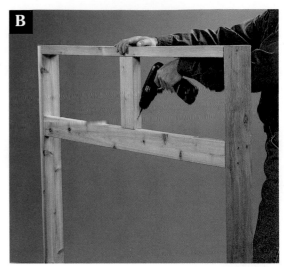

Drive deck screws toe-nail style through the braces and into the seat supports.

Directions: Trellis Seat

MAKE THE TRELLIS FRAMES. The trellis seat is constructed by joining two frames to a centrally-located post, then laying seat boards across the corner. Start by cutting the frame sides (A), frame bottoms (B), long rail (C), short rail (D), braces (K) and seat supports (L) from 2 × 4 cedar. Attach the frame sides to the frame bottoms with glue and two evenly-spaced 2½" deck screws, driven through counterbored ⅜6"-dia. pilot holes at the tops and bottoms of the frame sides. Attach the long and short rails to the tops of the frame sides with glue and deck screws driven through pilot holes in the top faces of the rails, and into the ends of the frame sides. The long rail should extend 3½" past one end of the frame **(photo A)**. Measure and mark points 22¼" from each end on the frame bottoms to indicate position for the spacers. Position the braces flush with the inside frame bottom edges, and attach the pieces by driving 3" deck screws through pilot holes in the frame bottoms and into the ends of the braces. Position the seat supports 16" up from the bottoms of the frame bottoms, resting on the braces. Make sure the seat supports are flush with the inside edges of the braces, then attach with glue and counterbored 3" deck screws driven through the frame sides and into the ends of the seat supports. Finally, attach the braces to the seat supports by drilling angled ⅜6"-dia. pilot holes through each brace

Fasten the trellis frames to the post at right angles.

edge. Drive 3" deck screws toe-nail style through the braces and into the top edges of the seat supports **(photo B).**

JOIN THE TRELLIS FRAMES TO THE POST. Now, connect the two trellis frames to the 4 × 4 post. Cut the post (I) to length. Attach the two frame sections to the post by driving evenly spaced, counterbored 3" deck screws through the frame sides into the post **(photo C).** Make sure the overhang of the long rail fits snugly over the top of the post.

Nail 1 × 2 retaining strips for the lattice panels to the inside faces of the trellis frames.

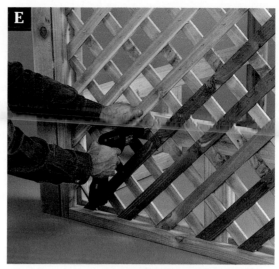

Fasten the lattice panels to the seat supports with 1¼" deck screws, then attach outer retaining strips.

ATTACH THE LATTICE RETAINING STRIPS. The 1 × 2 lattice retaining strips (H) hold the lattice panels in place in the trellis frames. Cut retaining strips to fit along the inside faces of the trellis frames (but not the seat supports or braces). Nail the strips to the frames, flush with the inside frame edges, using 4d galvanized casing nails **(photo D).**

CUT & INSTALL THE LATTICE PANELS. Cutting the lattice panels is a simple procedure. Since you will probably be cutting through some metal fasteners in the lattice, fit your circular saw with a remodeler's blade. Sandwich the lattice panel between two boards near the cutting line to prevent the lattice from separating. Clamp the boards and the panel together, and cut the lattice panels to size. Always wear protective eyewear when operating power tools. Position the panels into the frames against the retaining strips, and attach them to the seat supports with 1¼" deck screws **(photo E).** Secure the panels by cutting re-taining strips to fit along the outer edges of the inside faces of the trellis frame, then nailing the retaining strips in place.

BUILD THE SEAT. Cut the seat boards (J) from three pieces of 2 × 8 cedar. On a flat work surface, lay the seat boards together, edge-to-edge. Insert ½"-wide spacers between the boards, creating ½"-wide gaps. Draw cutting lines to lay out the seat shape onto the boards as if they were one board (see *Seat Detail,* page 15, for seat board dimensions). Gang-cut the seat boards to their finished size and shape with a circular saw. Attach the seat boards to the seat supports with evenly-spaced deck screws, maintaining the ½"-wide gap. Smooth the edges of the seat boards with a sander or router.

INSTALL TOP CAPS. The cap boards create handy shelves at the tops of the trellis frames. Cut the short cap (F) and long cap (G), then attach the caps to the tops of the long and short rails with deck screws **(photo F).**

APPLY FINISHING TOUCHES. We simply brushed on a coat of clear wood sealer to help preserve our project.

Attach the long and short caps to the tops of the trellis frames. The long cap overlaps the long rail and the post.

17

Outdoor Storage Center

*Create additional storage space for backyard games and equipment
with this efficient outdoor storage center.*

CONSTRUCTION MATERIALS

Quantity	Lumber
2	⅝" × 4 × 8' textured cedar plywood siding
2	¾" × 2 × 4' BC fir plywood handy panels
2	1 × 2" × 8' cedar
6	1 × 3" × 8' rough-sawn cedar
2	1 × 4" × 8' rough-sawn cedar
1	2 × 2" × 8' pine
1	1 × 2" × 8' pine

Sturdy cedar construction and a rustic appearance make this storage center an excellent addition to any backyard or outdoor setting. The top lid flips up for quick and easy access to the upper shelf storage area, while the bottom doors swing open to grant access to the lower storage compartments. The raised bottom shelf keeps all stored items up off the ground where they stay safe and dry. Lawn chairs, yard games, grilling supplies, fishing and boating equipment, and much more, can be easily kept out of sight and protected from the weather. If security is a concern, simply add a locking hasp and padlock to the top lid to keep your life jackets and horseshoe games safe from unwanted guests. If you have a lot of traffic in and out of the top compartment, add lid support hardware to prop the lid open.

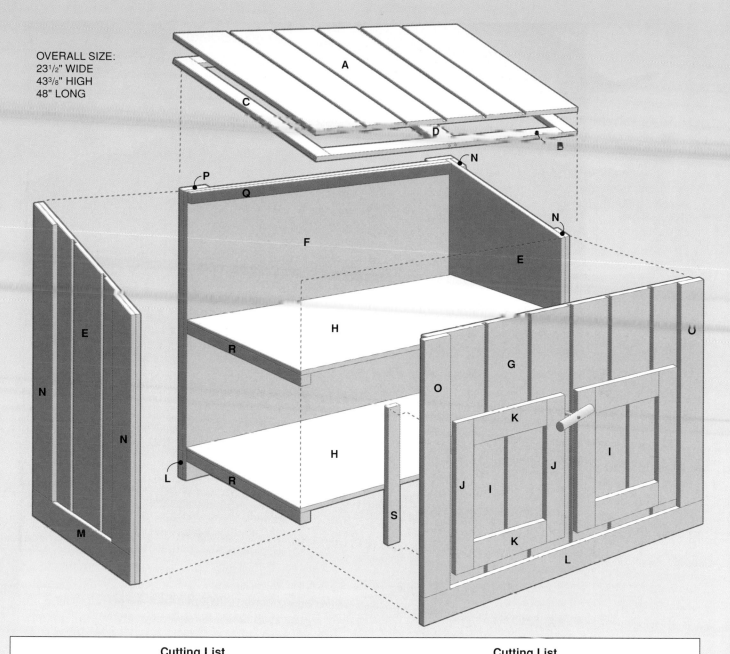

OVERALL SIZE:
23¹/₂" WIDE
43³/₈" HIGH
48" LONG

Cutting List

Key	Part	Dimension	Pcs.	Material	Key	Part	Dimension	Pcs.	Material
A	Lid	⅝ × 24 × 48"	1	Plywood siding	K	Door rail	¾ × 3½ × 12¼"	4	Cedar
B	Lid edge	¾ × 1½ × 45"	2	Cedar	L	Kickboard	¾ × 2½ × 47½"	2	Cedar
C	Lid end	¾ × 1½ × 24"	2	Cedar	M	End plate	¾ × 2½ × 22"	2	Cedar
D	Lid stringer	¾ × 2½ × 21"	1	Cedar	N	End trim	¾ × 2½ × 39½"	4	Cedar
E	End panel	⅝ × 22 × 42"	2	Plywood siding	O	Front trim	¾ × 2½ × 35"	2	Cedar
F	Back panel	⅝ × 44¾ × 42"	1	Plywood siding	P	Back trim	¾ × 2½ × 39½"	2	Cedar
G	Front panel	⅝ × 44¾ × 37½"	1	Plywood siding	Q	Hinge cleat	¾ × 1½ × 44¾"	1	Pine
H	Shelf	¾ × 20¾ × 44¾"	2	Fir plywood	R	Shelf cleat	1½ × 1½ × 20¾"	4	Pine
I	Door panel	⅝ × 15¾ × 17¾"	2	Plywood siding	S	Door cleat	¾ × 1½ × 18"	2	Pine
J	Door stile	¾ × 3½ × 21¼"	4	Cedar					

Materials: Moisture-resistant glue, (6) hinges, deck screws (1¼", 2½"), (2) door catches or a 1" dia. × 12" dowel and a ¼"-dia. × 4" carriage bolt, finishing materials.

Note: All measurements reflect actual size of dimensional lumber.

19

Cut and fasten the lid to the lid framework with the grooves in the panel running back to front.

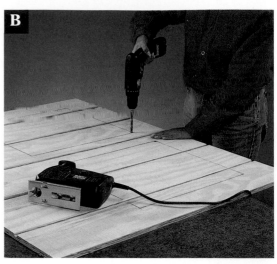

Drill a ⅜"-dia. starter hole at a corner of each door opening and cut out the openings with a jig saw.

Directions: Outdoor Storage Center

MAKE THE LID ASSEMBLY. Start by cutting the lid (A) from cedar sheet siding (we used siding with 8"-on-center channels) using a circular saw and a straightedge. Cut the lid edges (B) from 1 × 2 cedar, and cut the lid stringer (D) from 1 × 3 cedar. Lay the lid ends and edges on their faces, smooth side up, on a flat surface. Position the lid ends flush with the outsides of the lid edges. Fasten with glue and 2½" deck screws. Position the lid stringer midway between the lid ends, and glue and screw it in place. Apply glue to the top faces of the lid end, stringer, and lid edges. Set the lid on the frame assembly **(photo A)** and screw it in place with 1¼" deck screws.

MAKE THE PANELS. Start by cutting the back panel (F) and front panel (G) to size from cedar sheet siding. On the inside face of the front panel, measure up from the bottom and scribe straight lines at 5" and 23". Also measure in 4"

Attach the end panels to the back panel, keeping the back panel flush with the back edges of the end panels.

and 22" from each side and scribe lines. These square layout lines mark the cutout lines for the door openings. Next, drill a ⅜"-dia. starter hole at one corner in each door opening **(photo B).** Cut out the door openings with a jig saw and sand the edges smooth. Cut the end panels (E) to size. On the front edge of each panel, measure down 4½" and place a mark. Draw a line connecting each mark with the top corner on the back edge of the panel, creating cross-cutting lines for

the back-to-front tapers on the side panels. Cross-cut along the lines with a circular saw.

CREATE THE PANEL ASSEMBLY. Stand the back panel on its bottom edge and butt it up between the end panels, flush with the back edges. Fasten the back panel between the side panels with glue and 1¼" screws **(photo C).**

BUILD & ATTACH THE SHELVES. Cut the shelves (H) to size from plywood. Measure up 25" from the bottoms of the end panels and draw reference marks for

Place the shelf on top of the cleats and fasten with glue and screws.

positioning the top shelf. Cut the shelf cleats (R) from 2 × 2 cedar. Attach the cleats just below the reference lines with glue and 1¼" screws driven through the end panels and into the cleats. Fasten the shelf to the cleats with 1¼" screws **(photo D).** Also drive screws through the back panel and into the back edge of the shelf. Mark reference lines for the bottom shelf, 4" up from the bottoms of the side panels. Install the bottom shelves the same way as the top shelves. Position the front panel (G) between the end panels and fasten with glue and screws.

CUT & INSTALL TRIM. Cut the kickboards (L) for the front and back, the end plates (M), the end trim (N), the front trim (O), and the back trim (P) from 1 × 3 rough-sawn cedar. Sand all ends smooth. Attach the end kick boards at the bases of the side panels, using counterbored deck screws. Next, attach the front and back kickboards to the bases of the front and back panels. Hold the end trim pieces in position against the side panels at both the front and back edges, and trace the profile of the tapered side panels onto the trim pieces to make cutting lines (the trim pieces at the fronts should be flush with the front panel). Cut at the lines with a circular saw. Screw the end trim pieces to the side panels **(photo E).** Attach the front and back trim to the front and back panels, covering the edges of the end trim pieces.

ATTACH THE DOORS & LID. Cut the door stiles and door rails to size from 1 × 4 cedar, then attach them to the cutout door panels (I), forming a frame that extends 1¾" past the edges of the door panels on all sides. Cut 1 × 2 door cleats (S) to size and screw them to the inside faces of the front panel directly behind the hinge locations at the outside edges of the openings. Mount two butt hinges on the outside edge of each door, then screw the hinges to the front panel and hinge cleats. Install a door catch for each door (instead, we used a 1" dowel bolted to the front panel as a turnbuckle—see page 19). Mount the lid to the back panel and cleat with butt hinges.

APPLY FINISHING TOUCHES. Sand all edges smooth, then apply a coat of clear wood sealer, or any other finish of your choice.

Attach the end trim to the end panel, keeping the front edge of the trim flush with the face of the front panel.

Porch Swing

*You'll cherish the pleasant memories created
by this porch swing built for two.*

CONSTRUCTION MATERIALS

Quantity	Lumber
8	1 × 2" × 8' pine
1	1 × 4" × 4' pine
2	2 × 4" × 10' pine
1	2 × 6" × 10' pine

Nothing conjures up pleasant images of a cool summer evening like a porch swing. When the porch swing is one that you've built yourself, the images will be all the more pleasant. Our porch swing is made from sturdy pine to withstand years and years of memory making. The gentle curve of the slatted seat and the relaxed angle of the swing back are designed for your comfort. When you build your porch swing, pay close attention to the spacing of the rope holes drilled in the back, arms and seat of the swing. They are arranged to create perfect balance when you hang your swing from your porch ceiling.

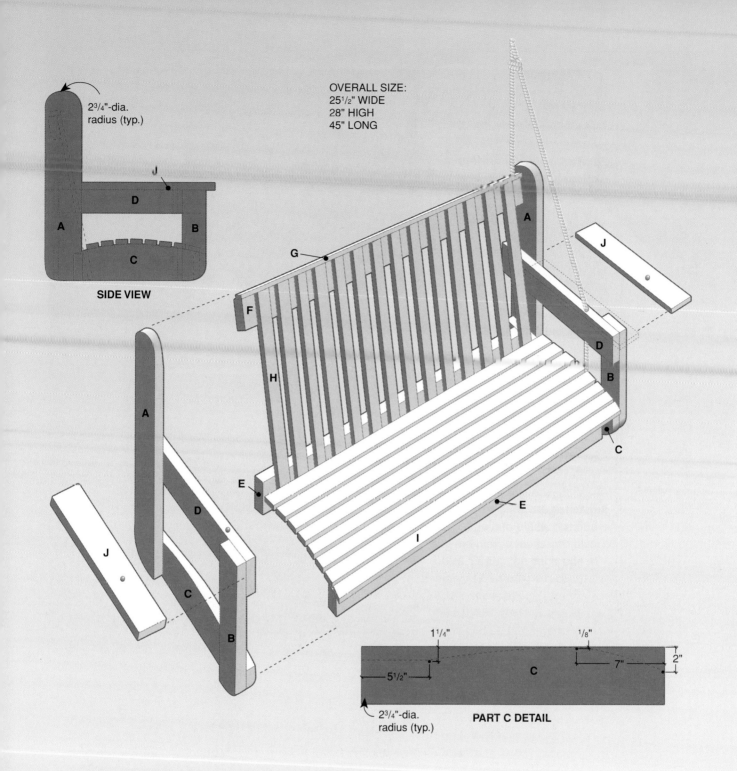

2³/₄"-dia.
radius (typ.)

SIDE VIEW

OVERALL SIZE:
25½" WIDE
28" HIGH
45" LONG

1¹/₄"   1/₈"
5½"   7"   2"

2³/₄"-dia.
radius (typ.)

PART C DETAIL

Cutting List

Key	Part	Dimension	Pcs.	Material
A	Back upright	1½ × 5½ × 28"	2	Pine
B	Front upright	1½ × 3½ × 13½"	2	Pine
C	Seat support	1½ × 5½ × 24"	2	Pine
D	Arm rail	1½ × 3½ × 24"	2	Pine
E	Stretcher	1½ × 3½ × 39"	2	Pine

Cutting List

Key	Part	Dimension	Pcs.	Material
F	Back cleat	1½ × 3½ × 42"	1	Pine
G	Top rail	¾ × 1½ × 42"	1	Pine
H	Back slat	¾ × 1½ × 25"	14	Pine
I	Seat slat	¾ × 1½ × 42"	8	Pine
J	Arm rest	¾ × 3½ × 20"	2	Pine

Materials: Wood glue, 20' of ½"-dia. nylon rope, wood screws (#8 x 2", #10 x 2½", #10 x 3").

Note: Measurements reflect the actual size of dimensional lumber.

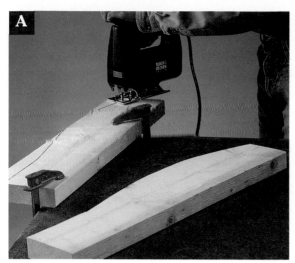

Use a jig saw to cut the contours into the tops of the seat supports.

Use a ⅜" spade bit and a right-angle drilling guide when drilling rope holes through the seat supports.

Directions: Porch Swing

MAKE THE SEAT SUPPORTS. Cut the seat supports (C) from 2 × 6 stock. Use the pattern on page 23 as a pattern for laying out the contour on the top of one of the seat supports. Use a flexible ruler, bent to follow the contour, to ensure that the cutting line is smooth (see page 12). Cut along the cutting line with a jig saw **(photo A).** Sand the contour smooth with a drill and drum sander or with a belt sander, then use the contoured seat support as a template for marking a matching contour on the other seat support. Cut and sand the second seat support to match.

BUILD THE SEAT FRAME. Cut the arm rails (D), and stretchers (E) from 2 × 4 pine. Attach one of the stretchers between the seat supports, ¾" from the front edges and ½" from the bottom edges, using glue and #10 × 2½" wood screws. Fasten the other stretcher between the supports so the front face of the stretcher is 6" from the backs of the supports, and all bottom edges are flush. Use a ⅝" spade

Smooth out the top exposed edges of the seat slats with a router and ¼" roundover bit (or use a power sander).

bit to drill guide holes for the ropes in the seat supports and the arm rails. Drill a hole 1½" from the back end of each piece, and also drill a hole 4½" from the front end of each piece. Use a right-angle drill guide to make sure holes stay centered all the way through **(photo B).**

INSTALL THE SEAT SLATS. Cut the seat slats (I) from 1 × 2 pine (make sure to buy full-sized 1 × 2s, not 1 × 2 furring strips). Arrange the slats across the seat supports, using ½"-thick spacers to make sure the gaps are even. The front slat should

overhang the front stretcher by about ¼", and the back slat should be flush with the front of the back stretcher. Fasten the slats to the seat support with glue and #8 × 2" wood screws (one screw at each slat end). Smooth the top edges of the slats with a router and ¼" roundover bit, or a power sander **(photo C).**

BUILD THE BACK. Cut the back cleat (F) from 2 × 4 pine, and cut the back slats (H) from 1 × 2 pine. Fasten the slats to the back cleat, leaving a 1½" gap at each end, and spacing the slats at regular 1½" intervals

Use 1 × 2 spacers to align the back slats, then fasten the slats to the back cleat.

Fasten the top rail to the back cleat, so the front edge of the rail is flush with the fronts of the slats.

Slide the back assembly against the seat assembly and attach.

(photo D). The tops of the slats should be flush with the top of the cleat. Cut the top rail (G) from 1 × 2 pine, and fasten it to the cleat so the front edge of the rail is flush with the fronts of the slats **(photo E).** Drill a ⅝"-dia. rope hole at each end of the top cleat, directly over the back holes in the arm rails.

ATTACH UPRIGHTS & ARM REST. Cut the back uprights (A) from 2 × 6 pine, and cut the front uprights (B) from 2 × 4 pine. Make a round profile cut at the tops of the back uprights (pattern, page 23), using a jig saw. Attach the uprights to the outside faces of the seat supports, flush with the ends of the supports. Use glue and two #10 × 3" wood screws at each joint. Slide the back slat assem-

bly behind the seat assembly **(photo F),** and screw the back cleat to the back uprights, so the upper rear corners of the cleat are flush with the back edges of the uprights. Attach the arm rails between the uprights, flush with the tops. Make sure the rope holes are aligned. Cut the arm rest (J) from 1 × 4 pine, then smooth the edges. Set the arm rests on the arm rail, centered side to side and flush against the back uprights. Mark the locations of the rope holes in the arm rails onto the arm rests, then drill matching holes into the arm rests. Attach arm rests to rails with glue and #8 × 2" screws.

APPLY FINISHING TOUCHES. Sand and paint the swing, then thread pieces of ½"-dia. nylon rope through all four sets of rope holes (see photo, page 22) and tie them to hang the swing.

TIP

Use heavy screw eyes driven into ceiling joists to hang porch swings. If the ropes don't line up with the ceiling joists, lag screw a 2 × 4 cleat to the ceiling joists and attach screw eyes to the cleat.

Freestanding Arbor

Create a shady retreat on a sunny patio or deck with this striking arbor. The design features an Oriental flavor that will bring a taste of the exotic to any setting. So park your favorite bench or chair under the sheltering cedar of this arbor and let the relaxation begin.

This freestanding arbor combines the beauty and durability of natural cedar with an Oriental-inspired design. Set it up on your patio or deck, or in a quiet corner of your backyard, to add just the right finishing touch to turn your outdoor living space into a showplace geared for relaxation and quiet contemplation. The arbor has a long history as a focal point in gardens and other outdoor areas throughout the world. And if privacy and shade are concerns, you can enhance the sheltering quality by adding climbing vines that weave their way in and out of the trellis. Or simply set a few potted plants around the base to help the arbor blend in with the outdoor environment. Another way to integrate plantlife into your arbor is to hang decorative potted plants from the top beams.

This arbor is freestanding, so it can be moved to a new site easily whenever you desire. Or, you can anchor it permanently to a deck or to the ground and equip it with a built-in seat. Sturdy posts made from 2 × 4 cedar serve as the base of our arbor, forming a framework for a 2 × 2 trellis system that scales the sides and top. The curved cutouts that give the arbor its Oriental appeal are made with a jig saw, then smoothed out with a drill and drum sander for a more finished appearance.

Quantity	Lumber
2	1 × 2" × 8' cedar
5	2 × 2" × 8' cedar
9	2 × 4" × 8' cedar
3	2 × 6" × 8' cedar

CONSTRUCTION MATERIALS

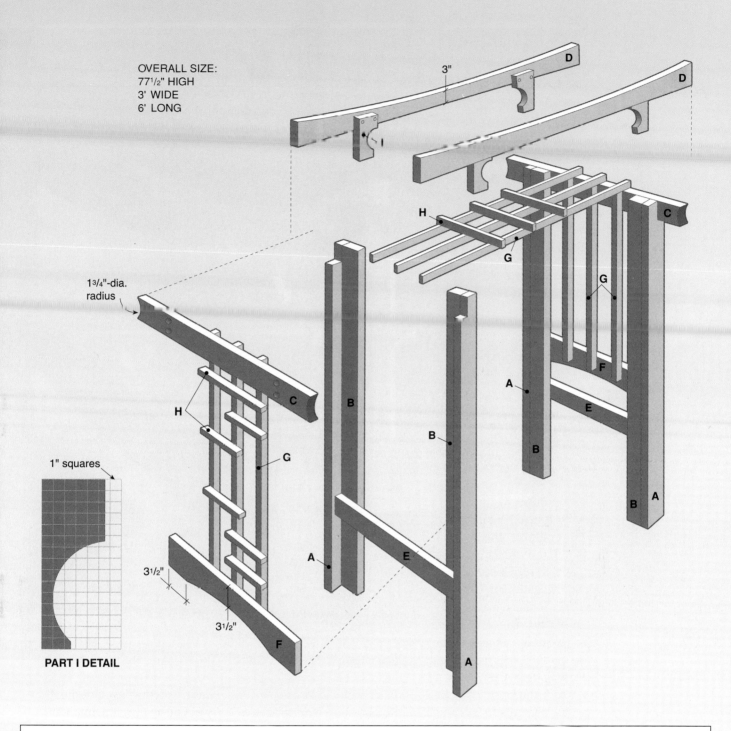

OVERALL SIZE:
77½" HIGH
3' WIDE
6' LONG

3"

1¾"-dia.
radius

1" squares

3½"

3½"

PART I DETAIL

Cutting List						Cutting List				
Key	Part	Dimension	Pcs.	Material		Key	Part	Dimension	Pcs.	Material
A	Leg front	1½ × 3½ × 6'	4	Cedar		F	Side spreader	1½ × 5½ × 21"	2	Cedar
B	Leg side	1½ × 3½ × 6'	4	Cedar		G	Trellis strip	1½ × 1½ × 4'	9	Cedar
C	Cross beam	1½ × 3½ × 3'	2	Cedar		H	Cross strip	¾ × 1½ × *	15	Cedar
D	Top beam	1½ × 5½ × 6'	2	Cedar		I	Brace	1½ × 5½ × 15"	4	Cedar
E	Side rail	1½ × 3½ × 21"	2	Cedar						

Materials: Wood glue, wood sealer or stain, #10 × 3" wood screws, deck screws (1¼", 2½"), finishing materials,

Note: Measurements reflect the actual size of dimensional lumber.

* Cut to fit

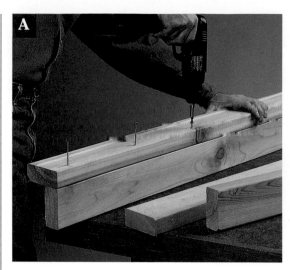

Create four legs by fastening leg sides to leg fronts at right angles.

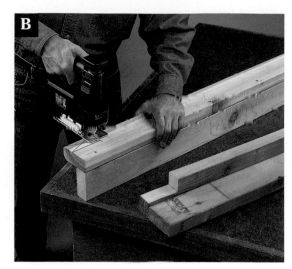

Cut a notch in the top of each of the four legs to hold the cross beams.

Directions: Freestanding Arbor

MAKE THE LEGS. Each of the four arbor legs is made from two 6'-long pieces of 2 × 4 cedar, fastened at right angles with 3" deck screws. Cut the leg fronts (A) and leg sides (B), and position the leg sides and fronts so the top and bottom edges are flush. Apply moisture-resistant glue to the joint, and attach the leg fronts to the leg sides with evenly spaced screws driven through the faces of the fronts and into the edges of the sides **(photo A).** Then, use a jig saw to cut a 3½"-long × 2"-wide notch at the top outside corner of each leg front **(photo B).** These notches are made to cradle the cross beams when the arbor is assembled.

MAKE THE CROSS BEAMS, RAILS & SPREADERS. Begin this step by cutting both cross beams (C) to

A piece of cardboard acts as a template when you trace the outline for the arc on the cross beams.

length from 2 × 4s. For a decorative touch, cut a small arc at both ends of each cross beam. Simply use a compass to draw a 3½"-diameter semicircle at the edge of a strip of cardboard, cut out the semicircle, and use the strip as a template for marking the arcs **(photo C).** Cut out the arcs with a jig saw, then sand the cuts smooth with a drill and drum sander. The rails (E) are also cut from 2 × 4s. They are fitted between pairs of legs on each side of the arbor, near the bottom, to keep the ar-

bor square. Cut them to length. Also cut two spreaders (F) from 2 × 6 cedar—the spreaders fit just above the rails on each side. After cutting the spreaders to length, mark a curved cutting line on the bottom of each spreader (see diagram, page 27). To mark the cutting lines, draw starting points 3½" in from each end of a spreader, then make a reference line 2" up from the bottom of the spreader board. Tack a casing nail on the refer-

Lag-screw the cross beams to the legs, and fasten the spreaders and rails with deck screws to assemble the side frames.

Attach trellis strips to the cross brace and spreader with deck screws.

boards are 21" apart. Set a cross beam into the notches, overhanging each leg by 6", and also set a spreader and a rail between the legs for spacing. Attach the cross beam to each leg with glue and two ⅜"-dia. × 2½" lag screws driven through counterbored pilot holes **(photo D).** Making sure to keep the legs parallel, use glue and countersunk 3" deck screws to fasten the rail and spreader between the legs. The top of the spreader should be 29½" up from the bottoms of the legs, and the top of the rail should be 18" up from the leg bottoms.

ATTACH THE SIDE TRELLIS PIECES. Our freestanding arbor contains a trellis on each side and at the top. Each side trellis is made from vertical strips of cedar 2 × 2 that are fastened to the side frames. Horizontal cross strips will be added later to create a decorative cross-hatching effect (page 31). Cut three vertical trellis strips (G) for each side frame, and attach them to the side frames so they are spaced 2⅜" apart, with the ends flush with the top of the cross beam **(photo E).** Use 2½" counterbored deck screws to attach the trellis strips to the cross beam and the spreader. Attach trellis strips to both side frames.

CUT & SHAPE THE TOP BEAMS. The top beams (D) link the two side frames, and feature a

ence line, centered between the ends of the spreader. With the spreader clamped to the worksurface, also tack nails into the worksurface next to the starting lines on the spreader. Slip a thin strip of metal or plastic between the casing nails so the strip bows out to create a smooth arc. Trace the arc onto the spreader, then cut along the line with a jig saw. Smooth out with a drum sander, then use

the first spreader as a template for marking and cutting the second spreader (see page 12).

ASSEMBLE THE SIDE FRAMES. Each side frame consists of a front and back leg, joined together by a rail, spreader and a cross beam. Begin by laying two leg assemblies parallel on a worksurface, with the notched board in each leg facing up. Space the legs so the inside faces of the notched

TIP

Drill counterbores for lag screws in two stages: first, drill a pilot hole for the shank of the screw; then, use the pilot hole as a center to drill a counterbore for the washer and screw head.

29

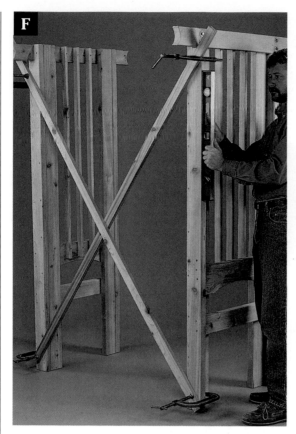

Use long pieces of 1 × 4 to brace the side frames in an upright, level position while you attach the top beams.

Lock the legs in a square position after assembling the arbor by tacking strips of wood between the front legs and between the back legs.

sweeping arc design. Cut two top beams to length from 2 × 6 cedar. Draw 1½"-deep arcs at the bottom edges of the top beams, starting at the ends of each board (see *Assemble the Side Frames*, page 31). Cut the arcs into the top beams with a jig saw, and sand smooth with a drum sander.

ASSEMBLE THE TOP & THE SIDES. Because the side frames are fairly heavy and bulky, you will need to brace them in an upright position in order to fasten the top beams between them. A simple way to accomplish this is to use a pair of 1 × 4 braces to connect the tops and bottoms of the side frames **(photo F).** Clamp the ends of the braces to the side frames so the side frames are 4' apart, and use a level to make sure the side frames are plumb. Then, mark a centerpoint for a lag bolt 12¾" from each end of each top beam, and drill a ¼"-diameter pilot hole through that centerpoint. Set the top beams on top of the cross braces of the side frames, and use a pencil to mark the pilot hole locations onto the cross

beams. Remove the top beams and drill pilot holes through the cross beams. Counterbore the pilot holes, then secure the top beams to the cross beams with 6" lag bolts and washers. Cut four braces (I) to size, and transfer the brace cutout pattern from the diagram on page 29 to each board. Cut the patterns with a jig saw, then attach the braces at the joints where the leg fronts meet the top beams, using 2½" deck screws. To make sure the arbor assembly stays in position while you complete the project, attach 1 × 2 scraps between the front legs and between the back legs **(photo G).** Cut and attach three trellis strips (G) between the top beams (see *Attach the Side Trellis Pieces*, page 31).

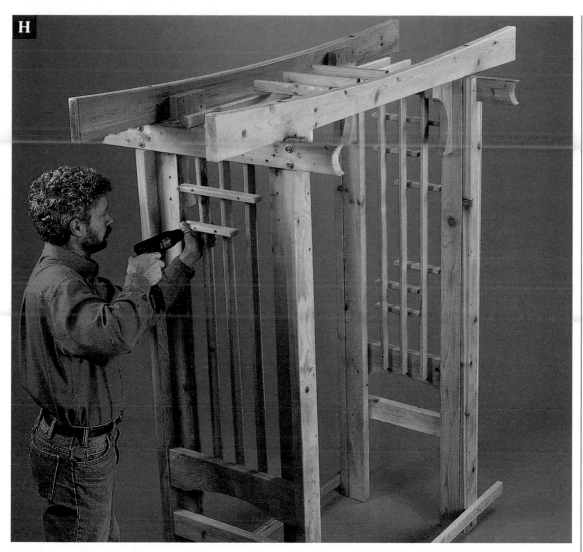

Attach the trellis cross strips to spice up the design and assist climbing plants.

ADD TRELLIS CROSS STRIPS. The 1 × 2 cross strips that fit between the trellis strips on the sides and top are an important part of our distinctive arbor design. We cut the cross strips to 7" and 10" lengths, and installed them at 3" intervals in a staggered pattern **(photo H).** Feel free to adjust the sizes and placement of the cross strips if you prefer. But for best appearance, try to retain some symmetry of placement between the cross strips, and make sure that the strips that fit across the top trellis strips are arranged similarly to the side strips.

APPLY THE FINISHING TOUCHES. To protect the arbor, coat the cedar wood with clear wood sealer. After the finish dries, the arbor is ready to be placed onto your deck or patio, or in a quiet corner of your yard. Because of its sturdy construction, the arbor can simply be set onto a hard, flat surface and it is ready to begin duty. If you plan to install a permanent seat in the arbor, you should anchor it to the ground. The best way to anchor it depends on the type of surface it is resting on. For decks, try to position the arbor so you can

screw the legs to the rim of the deck, or toenail the legs into the deck boards. You can buy fabricated metal post stakes, available at most building centers, to anchor the arbor to the ground.

> TIP
>
> *Create an arbor seat by resting two 2 × 10 cedar boards on the rails in each side frame. Overhang the rails by 6" or so, and drive a few 3" deck screws through the boards and into the rails to secure the seat.*

Play Center

With this portable play center, children can have fun storing and organizing their toys right where they play with them.

CONSTRUCTION MATERIALS

Quantity	Lumber
1	¾" × 4 × 8' plywood
1	2 × 4" × 6' pine

Provide toddlers and young children with a clean, safe, easily accessible storage and play area with this efficient, portable play center. Built at heights that are comfortable for kids, the top shelves are meant to be used as play surfaces—they can even be fitted with plastic containers to hold sand, water, blocks or dolls. This unit is completely portable, so you can roll it onto the deck, plant it under a favorite shade tree, or park it on the backyard patio. And if the weather is not cooperating, you can bring it indoors to the family room. The play center is so simple to make, you may want to have the kids chip in and help you build it.

32

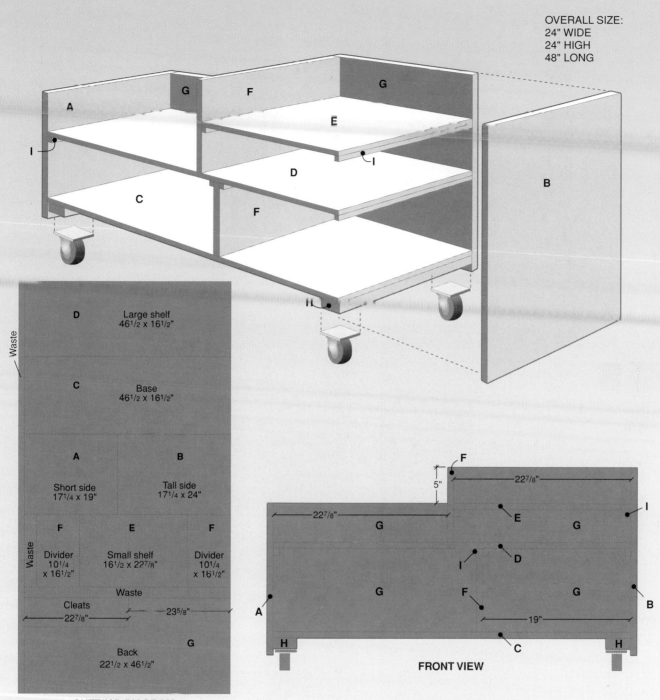

OVERALL SIZE:
24" WIDE
24" HIGH
48" LONG

CUTTING DIAGRAM

Waste

D — Large shelf 46½ x 16½"

C — Base 46½ x 16½"

A — Short side 17¼ x 19"

B — Tall side 17¼ x 24"

F — Divider 10¼ x 16½"

E — Small shelf 16½ x 22⅞"

F — Divider 10¼ x 16½"

Waste

Waste

Cleats — 22⅞" — 23⅝"

G — Back 22½ x 46½"

FRONT VIEW

5"

22⅞"

22⅞"

19"

Cutting List

Key	Part	Dimension	Pcs.	Material
A	Short side	¾ × 17¼ × 19"	1	MDO plywood
B	Tall side	¾ × 17¼ × 24"	1	MDO plywood
C	Base	¾ × 16½ × 46½"	1	MDO plywood
D	Large shelf	¾ × 16½ × 46½"	1	MDO plywood
E	Small shelf	¾ × 16½ × 22⅞"	1	MDO plywood

Cutting List

Key	Part	Dimension	Pcs.	Material
F	Divider	¾ × 16½ × 10¼"	2	MDO plywood
G	Back	¾ × 22½ × 46½"	1	MDO plywood
H	Base cleat	1½ × 3½ × 16"	2	Pine
I	Shelf cleat	¾ × ¾ × 16½"	6	MDO plywood

Materials: Moisture resistant glue, 1½" deck screws, tape measure, finishing materials, (4) locking casters.

Note: Measurements reflect the actual size of dimensional lumber.

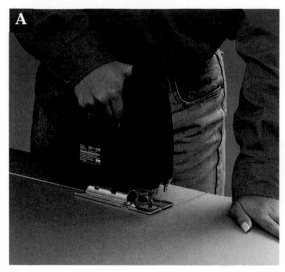

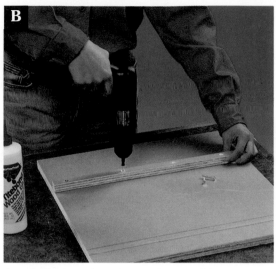

Use a jig saw to cut out a rectangular section of the back panel.

Attach cleats to the side panels at shelf locations.

Slip a divider between the base and the large shelf to support and compartmentalize the large shelf.

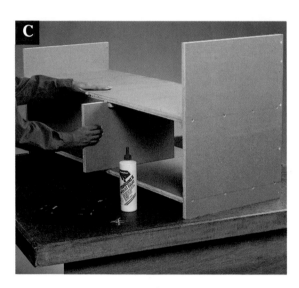

Directions: Play Center

CUT THE SIDES, BACK & BASE. Except for the 2 × 4 caster supports, the parts for the play center all are cut from one sheet of ¾"-thick MDO plywood, also known as "signboard." MDO plywood is coated on both faces with a special paper that produces a superior painted finish that stands up to exposure to the elements of nature. Use a circular saw and a straightedge guide to cut plywood panels. Start by cutting the short side (A), tall side (B), base (C) and back (G) from MDO plywood. The base and sides are square pieces that require no further cutting. The back needs to be cut into an L-shape. After cutting the back panel to full size (see *Cutting List*, page 35), make layout lines for a rectangular cutout at one corner. Measure out 5" from the corner on the short side of the panel, and measure out 22⅞" on the long side of the panel. Extend the marks out onto the face of the panel, using a square, then cut out along the lines to the point of intersection, using a jig saw **(photo A).** Remove the rectangular cutout and sand the edges of the cutout area.

ATTACH CLEATS TO PANELS. Cut a long strip of plywood from a waste area (see *Cutting Diagram*, page 35), then cut the strip into six 16½"-long pieces to use as shelf cleats. Mark reference lines at the shelf height on the short side and tall side panels: on the inside faces of each side panel, draw a straight line 13" up from the bottom edge to mark shelf-cleat height for the large shelf; draw another straight line 5¾" down from the top of the tall side panel to mark the shelf-cleat height for the small shelf. Attach a cleat (I) just below each of these marks, using glue and 1¼" counterbored deck screws **(photo B).** Cut the base cleats (H) from a 2 × 4. Mark reference lines for the cleats 2" up from the bottom edge of each side panel. Attach the base cleats just below the reference lines with glue and counterbored 3" deck screws driven through the outside faces of the side panels and into the edges of the cleats.

> **TIP**
>
> *Do not use coarse sandpaper on the faces of MDO plywood. Anything coarser than 100-grit can damage the paper facing.*

34

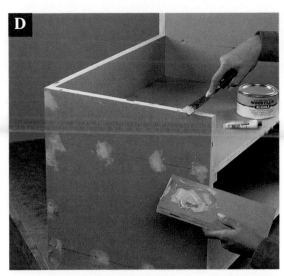

Fill screw holes and surface defects with exterior-rated wood filler or putty, then sand putty smooth.

Finish-sand the project with 220-grit sandpaper.

INSTALL THE BASE & LARGE SHELF. With the side panels propped in an upright position, set the base onto the base cleats so it is flush with the insides and front edges of the panels. Attach the base with glue and 1¼" counterbored deck screws driven through the outside faces of the side panels and into the edges of the base. Use four evenly spaced screws per side. Cut the large shelf (D), then set it on the shelf cleats on each side panel, making sure the front of the shelf is flush with the fronts of the side panels. Attach with glue and counterbored screws driven through the side panels and into the edges of the shelf.

ATTACH THE DIVIDERS. The dividers provide shelf support and create separate compartments within the play center for different kinds of toys or equipment. Cut the dividers (F). On one divider, mark a straight line 5¾" down from the top and install a shelf cleat for the small shelf just below the line. Glue two shelf cleats ¾" apart on the underside of the large shelf, cen-

tered around a mark 19" from the inside of the tall side panel. Once the glue dries, insert the cleatless divider between the cleats on the shelf **(photo C),** and attach with 1¼" deck screws driven through the shelf and base and into the edges of the divider. Attach the cleated divider to the top surface of the large shelf so the divider side with the cleat is 22⅞" away from the tall side panel. Cut the small shelf (E), set it on cleats on the top divider and the tall side panel, and attach it with deck screws. Now position the back panel so it fits between the side panels, flush against the back edges of the shelves and dividers. Drive counterbored deck screws through the back panel and into the dividers and shelves. Also drive counterbored 1¼" deck screws through the side panels and into the edges of the back panel.

COMPLETE THE PLAY CENTER. Fill screw holes and plywood voids with wood putty **(photo D).** Sand the putty until it is level with the surrounding surface **(photo E),** then finish-sand the entire project with 220-grit sandpaper. Wipe off the sanding residue with a rag dipped in mineral spirits, then apply a coat of exterior primer to all surfaces. After the primer dries, paint the play center with exterior paint that dries to an enamel finish **(photo F).** Attach a locking caster near both ends of each base cleat.

Prime and paint all surfaces on the play center.

Patio Chair

You won't believe how comfortable plastic tubes can be until you sit in this unique patio chair. It's attractive, reliable and very inexpensive to build.

For solid service, you can't go wrong with our patio chair. Crashing painfully to the ground just when you're trying to relax and enjoy the outdoors is nobody's idea of fun, so we designed this patio chair for durability and comfort. Our patio chair utilizes rigid plastic tubing for cool, comfortable support that's sure to last through many fun-filled seasons. Say good-bye to expensive or highly-specialized patio furniture with this outdoor workhorse.

This inventive seating project features CPVC plastic tubes that function like slats for the back and seat assemblies. The ½"-dia. tubes have just the right amount of flex and support, and can be purchased at any local hardware store. Even though the tubing is light, there is no danger of this chair blowing away in the wind. It has a heavy, solid frame that will withstand strong gusts of wind and fearsome summer showers. For even greater comfort, you can throw a favorite pillow, pad or blanket over the tubing and arms and relax in the sun.

The materials for this project are inexpensive. All the parts except the seat support are made from 2 × 4 cedar. The seat support is made from 1 × 3 cedar. For a companion project to this patio chair, see *Gate-Leg Picnic Tray,* pages 42 to 45.

CONSTRUCTION MATERIALS

Quantity	Lumber
3	2 × 4" × 10' cedar
1	1 × 3" × 2' cedar
7	½" × 10' CPVC tubing

OVERALL SIZE:
36" HIGH
26" WIDE
25" LONG

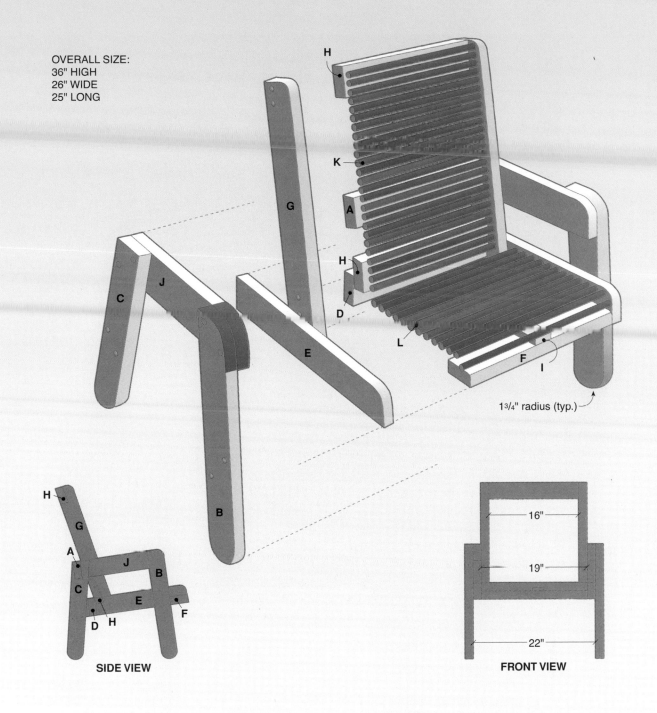

1³/₄" radius (typ.)

SIDE VIEW

16"

19"

22"

FRONT VIEW

Cutting List				
Key	**Part**	**Dimension**	**Pcs.**	**Material**
A	Back support	1½ × 3½ × 19"	1	Cedar
B	Front leg	1½ × 3½ × 22½"	2	Cedar
C	Rear leg	1½ × 3½ × 20½"	2	Cedar
D	Seat stop	1½ × 3½ × 19"	1	Cedar
E	Seat side	1½" × 3½ × 24½"	2	Cedar
F	Seat front	1½ × 3½ × 19"	1	Cedar

Cutting List				
Key	**Part**	**Dimension**	**Pcs.**	**Material**
G	Back side	1½ × 3½ × 28"	2	Cedar
H	Back rail	1½ × 3½ × 16"	2	Cedar
I	Seat support	¾ × 2½ × 17"	1	Cedar
J	Arm rail	1½ × 3½ × 19½"	2	Cedar
K	Back tube	½-dia. × 17½"	25	CPVC
L	Seat tube	½-dia. × 20½"	14	CPVC

Materials: Moisture-resistant glue, deck screws (1¼", 2½", 3"), ⅜"-dia. cedar plugs, finishing materials.

Note: Measurements reflect the actual size of dimensional lumber.

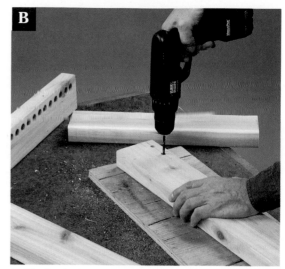

Use a portable drilling guide when drilling the holes for the tubes in the seat sides.

Drill pilot holes before attaching the back rails and sides.

Directions: Patio Chair

MAKE THE BACK SIDES. The first step in building the patio chair is constructing the back sides. The back sides provide the frame for the CPVC tubing. Make sure all cuts are accurate and smooth to achieve good, snug-fitting joints. Start by cutting the back sides (G) to length, using a circular saw. Your next step is to drill the stopped holes for the plastic tubes on the inside faces of the back sides. These holes must be accurately positioned and drilled, so use a pencil with either a combination square or a straight-edge to draw a centering line to mark the locations for the holes. Make the centering line ⅝" from the front edge of each back side. Drill ⅝-dia. × ¾"-deep holes, and center them exactly 1" apart along the centerline. Start the first hole 3" from the bottom end

Use a jig saw to cut the CPVC tubing slats. For stability, arrange the tubing so the saw blade is very close to the worksurface.

of each back side. Use a portable drilling guide and a square to make sure the holes are straight and perfectly aligned **(photo A).** A portable drilling guide fits easily onto your power drill to ensure quick and accurate drilling. Some portable drilling guides are even equipped with depth stops, making them the next best thing to a standard drill press.

BUILD THE BACK FRAME. Once the back sides have been cut and drilled, you can build

the back frame. Start by using a circular saw to cut the back rails (H) to size. These pieces will be attached to the inside faces of the back sides, flush with the back, top and bottom edges. To eliminate the sharp edges, clamp the pieces to a stable worksurface and use a sander or a router to soften the edges on the top and bottom of the back rails, and the top edges of the back sides. Dry-fit the back rails and back sides, and mark their positions with a

D

Attach the remaining side to complete the back assembly.

E

Attach the seat support to the seat front and seat lock as shown.

is usually available in 10' lengths. Use a jig saw to cut 25 pieces of the ½"-dia. CPVC tubing. Remember, these pieces will be used for the back seat assembly only; the seat assembly requires additional pieces. Cut the pieces to 17½" lengths **(photo C).** When you buy plastic tubing, you will find ink grade stamps imprinted on it every several inches along the outside. To make the patio chair more attractive, wash these grade stamps off with lacquer thinner. Always wear gloves and work in a well-ventilated area when using dangerous chemicals, like lacquer thinner. When the grade stamps have been removed, rinse the pipes with water. Once the pipes are clean and dry, insert them one-by-one into the holes on one of the back sides. Slide the remaining back side into place, positioning the plastic tubes into the holes. Fasten the back side to the side rails with glue and counterbored 3" deck screws **(photo D).**

BUILD THE SEAT FRAME. We designed and built the seat frame in much the same way as the back frame. One important difference is in the positioning of the CPVC tubing. On the seat frame, one tube is inserted into

pencil. Bore two ⅜"-dia. × ½"-deep holes into the outside faces of each back side. Make these holes where the back rails will be located. Drill ³⁄₁₆"-dia. pilot holes through the center of each hole **(photo B).** Apply moisture-resistant glue to one end of each rail and fasten them to a single back side with 3" deck screws.

COMPLETE THE BACK ASSEMBLY. Before you start assembling the back, you need to purchase and prepare the CPVC tubing for the frame holes. Make sure the tubing is ½"-dia. CPVC, which is rated for hot water. Standard PVC tubing is not usually sold in small diameters that will fit into the ⅜"-dia. holes you have drilled. This plastic tubing

TIPS

The easiest way to cut CPVC tubing is with a power miter box, but no matter what kind of saw you are using, remember to work in a well-ventilated room. Although plastic tubing generally cuts easily without melting or burning, it can release some toxic fumes as it is cut. When you're finished, you might consider treating the tubes with some automotive plastic polish to help preserve them.

the sides slightly out of line to make the chair more comfortable for your legs. Start by cutting the seat sides (E), seat front (F), seat stop (D) and seat support (I). Use the same methods as with the back frame to draw the centerling line for the plastic tubing. Drill the tube holes into each seat side. Start the holes 2" from the front end of the seat sides. Position a single tube hole on the seat frame ⅞" below the top edge, and 1" from the front end of each seat side. This front tube provides a gradual downward seat profile for increased leg comfort when you are seated. To eliminate the sharp edges on the seat assembly, round over the seat sides, seat support edges and seat front edges with a sander or router. Use a combination square to mark a line across the width of the inside of the seat sides, 3½" from the back edges. This is where the seat stop is positioned. Test-fit the pieces to make sure their positions are correct, then lay out and mark the position of the seat stop and seat front on each seat side. Carefully drill pilot holes in position to fasten one seat side, seat support and seat front as you did with the back rails. Connect the parts with moisture-resistant glue and deck screws.

COMPLETE THE SEAT FRAME. To complete the seat frame, you must attach the remaining seat side and fasten the seat support to the seat front and seat stop. The seat support (I) is located directly under the plastic tubing in the center of the seat and provides strength and support to the entire seat

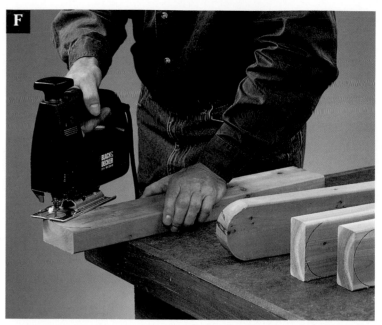

Make identical radius cuts on the bottoms of the legs.

Use a square to make sure the seat is perpendicular to the leg.

frame. Begin by cutting 14 pieces of ½"-dia. CPVC pipe. Each piece should be 20½" long. Once again, clean the grade stamps off the tubes with lacquer thinner, rinse them with clean water, and insert them into the holes on one seat side. Carefully slide the remaining seat side into place and fasten the pieces with moisture-

resistant glue and deck screws. Attach the seat support to the middle of the seat front and seat stop with moisture-resistant glue and 1¼" deck screws **(photo E).**

BUILD THE ARMS & LEGS. With the back and seat frames already constructed, the arms and legs are all that remain for

Slide the back frame into the seat frame so the back sides rest against the seat stop and seat support.

the excess material above the arm rail. More than any other, this part of the chair contacts your body, so make sure to round over and sand all the rough edges until they are completely smooth to the touch.

ATTACH THE BACK FRAME. Carefully slide the back frame into the seat frame so that the back sides rest against the seat stop **(photo H).** Make sure the back support and bottom of the back sides are flush with the bottom of the seat sides. Apply moisture-resistant glue, and attach the back frame by driving counterbored deck screws through the seat stop into the back rail.

APPLY THE FINISHING TOUCHES. For a fine decorative touch, apply glue to the bottoms of ⅜"-dia. cedar wood plugs, and insert them into the screw counterbores. Sand the tops of the plugs until they are even with the surrounding surface. Wipe the wood surfaces with a rag dipped in mineral spirits, then apply finishing materials. We used a clear wood sealer on the patio chair to preserve the look of the cedar.

the patio chair assembly. When you make the radius cuts on the bottom edges of the front and back legs, make sure the cuts are exactly the same on each leg (see *Diagram*, page 39). Otherwise, the legs may be uneven and rock back and forth when you sit down. Start by cutting the back support (A) and arm rails (J) to size. Fasten the back support between the arm rails with counterbored deck screws and glue. Be sure the back support is flush with the ends of the rails. Cut the front legs (B) and rear legs (C). Use a jig saw to cut a full radius on the bottoms of the legs **(photo F).** Attach the front legs to the outside of the arm rails so the legs are flush with the ends. It is very important to keep the front legs perpendicular to the arm rails.

ATTACH THE SEAT FRAMES. Attach the leg/arm rail assembly to the seat so that the top edge of the seat frame is 15" from the bottom of the leg. It is important to measure and mark accurately. Remember to position the front of the seat so that it extends exactly 3½" past the leg. Use a square to make sure the seat is perpendicular to the legs **(photo G).** Use glue and screws to fasten the rear legs to the arm rail and seat side so that the back edge of the leg is flush with the ends of the arm rail and seat side. Trim

TIP

When making the radius cuts on the bottom edges of the legs remember that when using a jig saw, it is tempting to speed up a cut by pushing the tool with too much force. Jig saw blades have a tendency to bend during curves, causing irregular cuts and burns. Since cedar is vulnerable to burning, be sure to make steady cutting passes. Curved cuts are easiest to make with multiple passes. Once the cuts have been made, sand the cut surfaces smooth.

Gate-leg Picnic Tray

Make outdoor dining on your porch, patio or deck a trouble-free activity with our picnic tray. Built with gate legs, it provides a stable surface for plates or glasses, yet folds up easily for convenient storage.

Outdoor dining doesn't need to be a messy, shaky experience. Whether you're on the lawn or patio, you can depend on our gate-leg picnic tray. A hinged leg assembly allows you to fold the tray for easy carrying and

storage. Two of the legs are fastened directly to supports beneath the main tray surface with hinges, while the third is attached only to the other legs, allowing it to swing back and forth like a gate and aid compact storage. A small wedge fits under the tray to prevent the swinging leg from moving once the tray is set up.

Our picnic tray also features a hinged bottom shelf that swings down and locks in place with a hook-and-eye clasp to keep the legs in place. Of course, the most conspicuous feature of the project is the tray surface. Plastic tubing is a

durable material, and it makes cleaning the tray top easy. The tubing also gives the project an interesting look—it's a companion piece to the patio chair on pages 36-41. Use a portable drill and drill stand to make the holes in the tray sides and insert the plastic tubing. CPVC tubing is a relatively lightweight material, but the strong cedar frame gives our project more stability than you'll get in conventional folding trays.

Even on grass, our gate-leg picnic tray will serve you well, allowing you to enjoy your meal without fear of a messy, dinnertime disaster.

CONSTRUCTION MATERIALS

Quantity	Lumber
1	1 × 2" × 12' cedar
1	1 × 3" × 6' cedar
1	1 × 4" × 8' cedar
1	1 × 12" × 2' cedar
4	½" × 10' CPVC tubing

OVERALL SIZE:
18" WIDE
22 3/8" HIGH
19" LONG

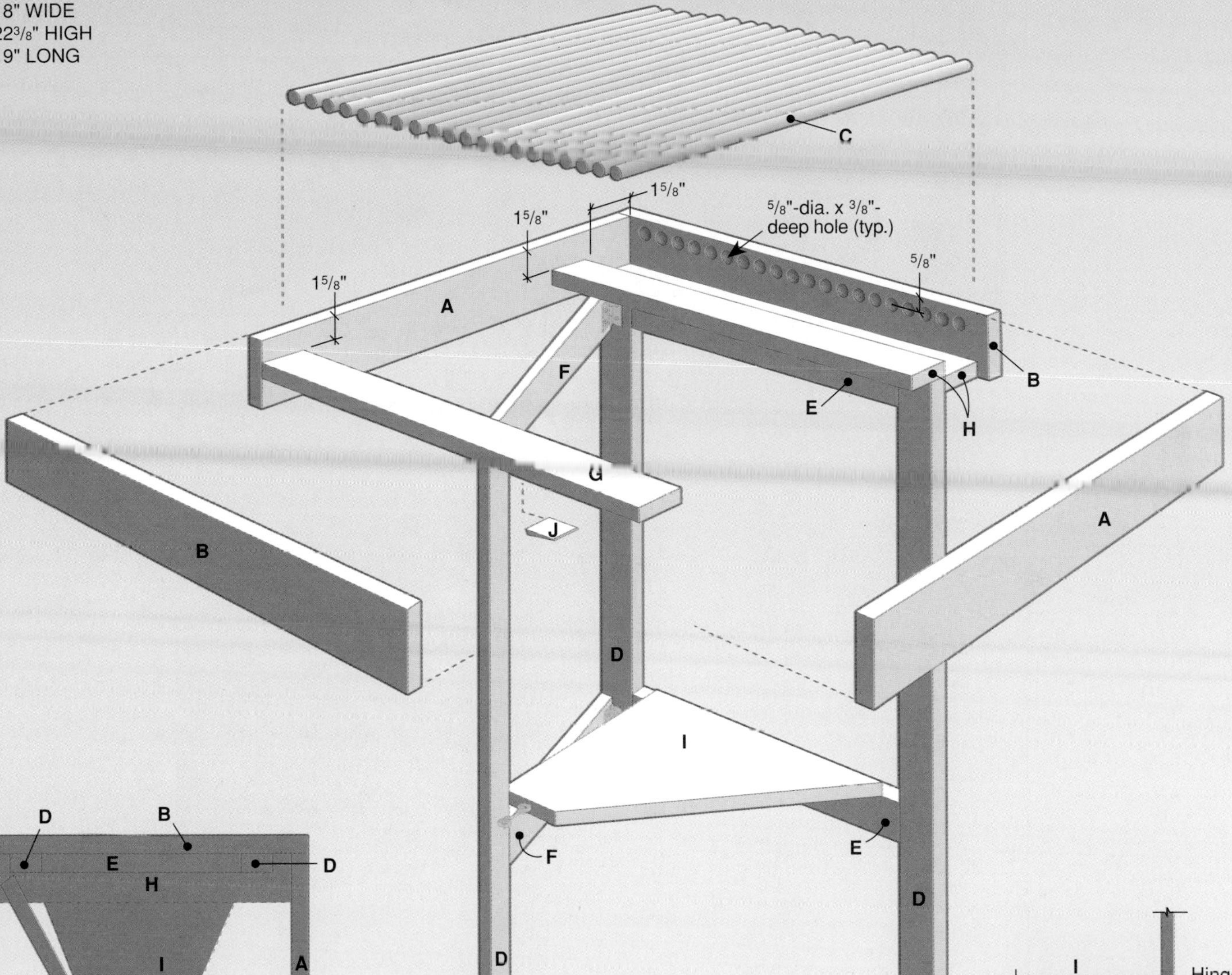

C
1 5/8"
1 5/8"
5/8"-dia. x 3/8"-deep hole (typ.)
5/8"
1 5/8"
A
F
B
E
H
G
J
B
A
D
I
F
E
D
D

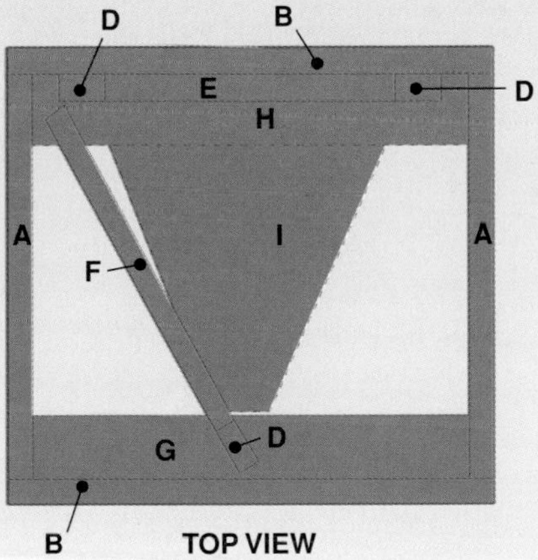

D
B
E
D
H
A
I
A
F
G
D
B

TOP VIEW

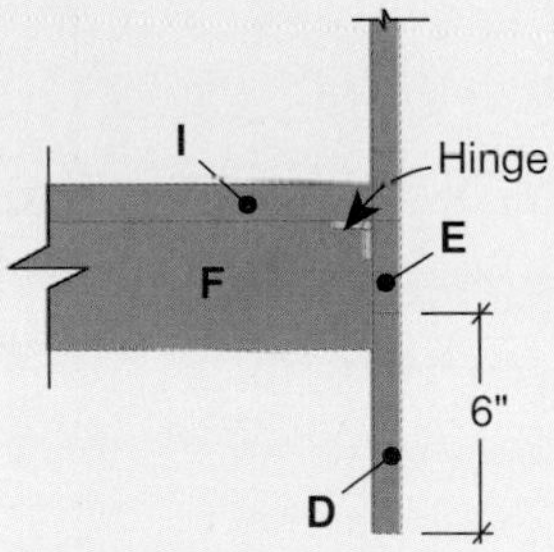

I
Hinge
E
F
6"
D

SIDE VIEW DETAIL

Cutting List

Key	Part	Dimension	Pcs.	Material
A	Side	¾ × 3½ × 16½"	2	Cedar
B	Cap	¾ × 3½ × 19"	2	Cedar
C	Tube	⅝"-dia. × 17¼"	20	CPVC
D	Leg	¾ × 1½ × 20"	3	Cedar
E	Short rail	¾ × 2½ × 13"	2	Cedar

Cutting List

Key	Part	Dimension	Pcs.	Material
F	Long rail	¾ × 1½ × 13½"	2	Cedar
G	Gate support	¾ × 2½ × 17½"	1	Cedar
H	Hinge support	¾ × 1½ × 17½"	2	Cedar
I	Shelf	1 × 10 × 12¾"	1	Cedar
J	Wedge	¼ × 2 × 2"	1	Cedar

Materials: Moisture-resistant glue, deck screws (1¼", 1½", 2", 3"), wire brads, exterior wood putty, hinges, finishing materials.

Note: Measurements reflect the actual size of dimensional lumber.

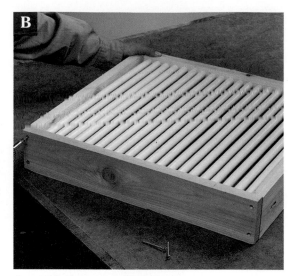

Clamp the pieces to hold them in place, and attach the hinge support 1⅝" from the top side edge.

Once the final cap has been attached with deck screws and glue, the basic tray frame is complete.

Directions:
Gate-Leg Picnic Tray

MAKE THE TRAY FRAME. First, construct the upper section of the project. It's a simple frame with stopped holes cut into the caps for the CPVC tubing. The underside of the tray frame is braced by supports, which provide a surface on which to anchor the legs. Begin by cutting the sides (A) and caps (B) to length from 1 × 4 cedar. Use a power drill to make ⅝ × ⅜"-deep holes for CPVC tubing, 1" apart in the inside faces of the caps. We recommend using a portable drill stand for this step (see *Tip*, below). Start the holes 1½" from one end and center

Attach the rails to the legs with counterbored deck screws and glue.

the holes ⅝" from the top cap edges. Cut the gate support (G) from 1 × 3 cedar and cut the hinge supports (H) from 1 × 2 cedar. Drill two evenly spaced ¼ × ⅜"-dia. counterbored holes into the outside face of the front end of each of the sides, where the gate support will be attached. Drill the holes 1⅝" down from the top edges of the sides. Apply moisture-resistant glue to the joints and clamp the piece with a bar clamp. Drill 3/16"-dia. pilot holes through each center, then fasten the

gate support to the sides with 2" deck screws. On the opposite side of the frame, fasten one hinge support between the sides **(photo A).** Make sure the hinge support is fastened 1⅝" from the ends of the sides, and 1⅝" from the top side edges. Fasten one of the caps to the side assembly with deck screws.

CUT & INSTALL THE TUBES. Use a jig saw or compound miter saw to cut 24 pieces of ½"-dia. CPVC tubing (C) to 17¼" in length. For more information on working with plastic tubing, see *Patio Table*, page 38-43.

Attach the leg frames with high quality hinges.

Fasten the stationary leg frame to the lower hinge support on the underside of the tray frame.

Use wire brads and glue to attach the lock wedge, which holds the gate leg assembly in place.

Wash the grade stamps from the tubing with lacquer thinner and rinse them with clean water. When the tubes are dry, insert the them into their holes in the frame. Fasten the remaining cap to the frame with glue and deck screws **(photo B).** Next, attach the remaining hinge support to the sides, starting ⅞" from the end on the outside edge. This hinge support should be flush with the bottom edges of the sides. Use glue and countersunk deck screws to attach the pieces.

BUILD THE LEG ASSEMBLY. The leg assembly consists of two leg

frames and a series of rails. One leg frame is stationary and is attached to the bottom hinge support with hinges. The other frame has only one leg, which swings like a gate and is attached only to the first frame. These braces are attached to the other leg frame. Begin the leg assembly by cutting the legs (D), short rails (E), and long rails (F) from 1 × 2 cedar. Fasten the rails to the legs (see *Diagram,* page 43) with counter-bored deck screws and glue to form two leg frames **(photo C).** The bottom edge of the rails should be 4" from the bottom

of the legs. The top rails should be flush with the top leg edges. Attach the gate leg frame to the stationary frame with hinges **(photo D),** then fasten the stationary legs to the bottom hinge support **(photo E).** To prevent the gate leg from swinging back and collapsing the assembled picnic tray, cut a lock wedge from 1 × 3 cedar. Open the gate leg to the normal standing position, which should be roughly the center of the gate support. Draw a line on the gate support along the edge of the gate leg to locate the wedge position. Use wire brads and glue to attach the lock wedge so that its thin end is against the gate leg **(photo F).** The leg will slide over this wedge slightly and be held fast. Cut the shelf (K) to size and shape. Attach it to the short rails with hinges. Install a hook-and-eye clasp on the gate leg and shelf to secure the open assembly. Sand all sharp edges and finish the project with clear wood sealer.

TIP

Use cedar plugs to fill the counter-bores for the screws in the tray frame.

Front-porch Mailbox

This cedar mailbox is a practical, good-looking project that is very easy to build. The simple design is created using basic joinery and mostly straight cuts.

If you want to build a useful, long-lasting item in just a few hours, our mailbox is the project for you. Replace that impersonal metal mailbox you bought at the hardware store with a distinctive cedar mailbox that is a lot of fun to build. The lines and design are so simple on this project that it

suits nearly any home entrance. Our mailbox features a hinged lid and a convenient lower shelf that is sized to hold magazines and newspapers.

We used select cedar to build our mailbox, then applied a clear, protective finish. Plain brass house numbers dress up the flat surface of the lid, which also features a decorative scallop that doubles as a handgrip.

If you are ambitious and economy-minded, you can build this entire mailbox using just one 8'-long piece of 1 × 10 cedar. That means, however, that you will have to do quite a bit of rip-cutting to make the

parts. If you have a good straightedge and some patience, rip-cutting is not difficult. But you may prefer to simply purchase dimensional lumber that matches the widths of the pieces (see the *Construction Materials* list to the left).

If your house is sided with wood siding, you can hang the mailbox by screwing the back directly to the siding. If you have vinyl or metal siding, be sure that the screws make it all the way through the siding and into wood sheathing or wood wall studs. If you have masonry siding, like brick or stucco, use masonry anchors to hang the mailbox.

CONSTRUCTION MATERIALS

Quantity	Lumber
1	1 × 10" × 4' cedar
1	1 × 8" × 4' cedar
1	1 × 4" × 3' cedar
1	1 × 3" × 3' cedar
1	1 × 2" × 3' cedar

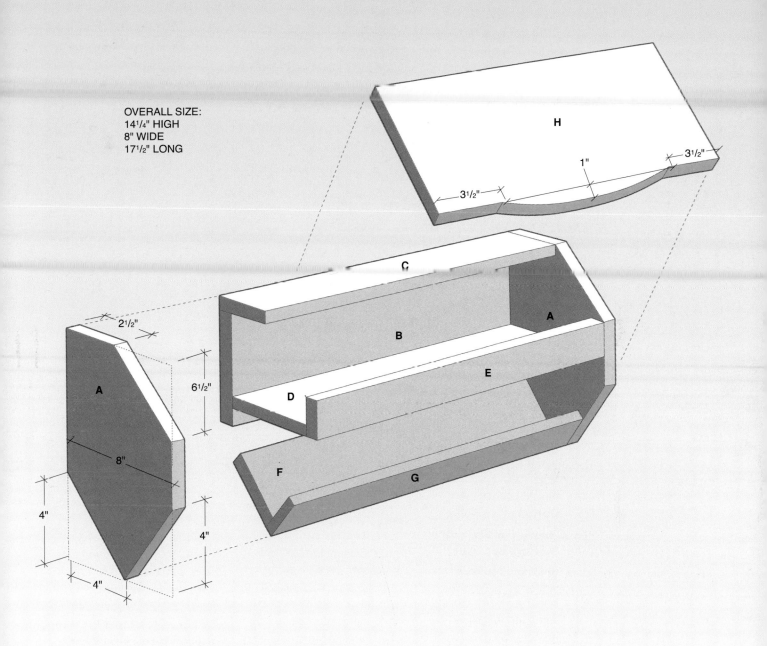

OVERALL SIZE:
14¼" HIGH
8" WIDE
17½" LONG

Cutting List						**Cutting List**			
Key	**Part**	**Dimension**	**Pcs.**	**Material**	**Key**	**Part**	**Dimension**	**Pcs.**	**Material**
A	Side	¾ × 8 × 14¼"	2	Cedar	**E**	Box front	¾ × 1½ × 16"	1	Cedar
B	Back	¾ × 7¼ × 16"	1	Cedar	**F**	Shelf bottom	¾ × 3½ × 16"	1	Cedar
C	Top	¾ × 2½ × 16"	1	Cedar	**G**	Shelf lip	¾ × 2½ × 16"	1	Cedar
D	Box bottom	¾ × 6½ × 16"	1	Cedar	**H**	Lid	¾ × 9¼ × 17½"	1	Cedar

Materials: Moisture-resistant wood glue, 2" deck screws, masking tape, continuous hinge, finishing materials.

Note: Measurements reflect the actual size of dimensional lumber.

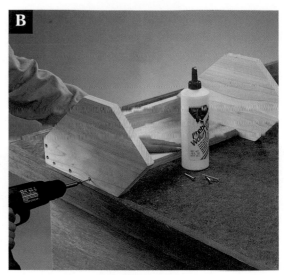

Cutlines are drawn on the sides, and the parts are cut to shape with a jig saw.

After fastening the top between the sides, fasten the back with deck screws.

Directions:
Front-porch Mailbox

BUILD THE SIDES. The sides are the trickiest parts to build in this mailbox design. But if you can use a ruler and cut a straight line, you should have no problems. First, cut two 8 × 14¼" pieces of ¾"-thick cedar to make the sides (A)—pieces of wood that will be shaped into parts are called "blanks" in the woodworkers' language. Next, lay out the cutting pattern onto one side blank, using the measurements shown on page 47. Mark all of the cutting lines, then double-check the dimensions to make sure the piece will be the right size when it is cut to shape. Make the cuts in the blank, using a jig saw, to create one side. Sand the edges smooth. Now, use the

Attach the bottom to the back with glue and screws driven through the back and sides.

side as a template to mark the second blank (this ensures that the two sides are identical). Try to arrange the template so the grain direction is the same in the blank and the template. Cut out and sand the second side **(photo A).**

ATTACH THE BACK & TOP. Use 2" deck screws and exterior wood glue to fasten all the pieces on the mailbox. Although cedar is a fine outdoor wood, it can be quite brittle, so drill pilot holes to prevent splitting the cedar edges, and space

the screws evenly when driving them into the pieces. Begin by cutting the back (B) and top (C) to size. Fasten the top between the 2½"-wide faces on the two sides. using glue and 2" deck screws. Position the top so that the rear face is flush with the rear side edges, and the top face is flush with the top side edges. Use glue and deck screws to fasten the back between the sides, flush with

TIPS

If you are planning on stenciling your name or address on the front of the mailbox, remember these helpful hints:

• Secure the stencil pattern to the surface with spray adhesive and drafting tape.

• Dip a stencil brush into the exterior latex paint, then wipe most of it off on a paper towel before painting.

• Let the paint dry thoroughly before removing the stencil.

Keep the lip edges flush with the side edges to form the newspaper shelf.

Once the pieces are taped in place, the continuous hinge is attached to join the lid to the top.

CUT & ATTACH THE LID. Begin by cutting the lid (H) to size (9¼" is the actual width of a 1 × 10). Draw a reference line parallel to and 1" away from one of the long edges. Use a jig saw to make a 3½"-long cut at each end of the line. Mark the midpoint of the edge (8¾"), then cut a shallow scallop to connect the cuts with the mid-point. Smooth out the cut with a sander. Attach a brass, 15"-long continuous hinge (sometimes called a "piano hinge") to the top edge of the lid. Then position the lid so the other wing of the hinge fits squarely onto the top of the mailbox. Secure the lid to the mailbox with masking tape, then attach the hinge to the mailbox **(photo F).**

APPLY THE FINISHING TOUCHES. Sand all the surfaces until they are completely smooth with 150-grit sandpaper, then finish the mailbox as desired. We used clear wood sealer. We also added 3" brass house numbers on the lid, but you may prefer to stencil an address or name onto the lid (see *Tip,* page 48). Once the finish has dried, hang the mailbox on the wall by driving screws through the back (see page 48).

> ### TIP
>
> *Clear wood sealer can be refreshed if it starts to yellow or peel. Wash the wood with a strong detergent, then sand the surface lightly to remove flaking or peeling sealer. Wash the surface again, then simply brush a fresh coat of sealer onto the wood.*

the 8"-long edges **(photo B),** and butted against the top.

ATTACH THE BOX BOTTOM & FRONT. Once assembled, the bottom and front pieces form the letter compartment inside the mailbox. Start by cutting the bottom (D) and front (E). Fasten the bottom to the back and sides, making sure the bottom edges are flush **(photo C).** Once the bottom is attached, fasten the front to the sides and bottom, keeping the bottom edges flush.

ATTACH THE NEWSPAPER SHELF. The lower shelf on the underside of the mailbox is designed for overflow mail, especially magazines and newspapers. To make the lower shelf, cut the shelf bottom (F) and shelf lip (G) to size. Fasten the shelf bottom to the leg of the "V" formed by the sides that is closer to the back. Fasten the shelf lip to the sides along the front edges to complete the shelf assembly **(photo D).**

Sun Lounger

Designed for the dedicated sun worshipper, this sun lounger has a
backrest that can be set in either a flat or an upright position.

CONSTRUCTION MATERIALS

Quantity	Lumber
3	2 × 2" × 8' pine
1	2 × 4" × 8' pine
5	2 × 4" × 10' pine
2	2 × 6" × 10' pine

Leave your thin beach towel and flimsy plastic chaise lounge behind as you relax and soak up the sun in this solid wood sun lounger. Set the adjustable backrest in an upright position while you make your way through your summer reading list. Then, for a change of pace, set the back-rest in the flat position and drift off in a pleasant reverie. If you are an ambitious suntanner, take comfort in the fact that this sun lounger is lightweight enough that it can be moved easily to follow the path of di-rect sunlight. Made almost en-tirely from inexpensive pine or cedar, this sun lounger can be built for only a few dollars— plus a little sweat equity.

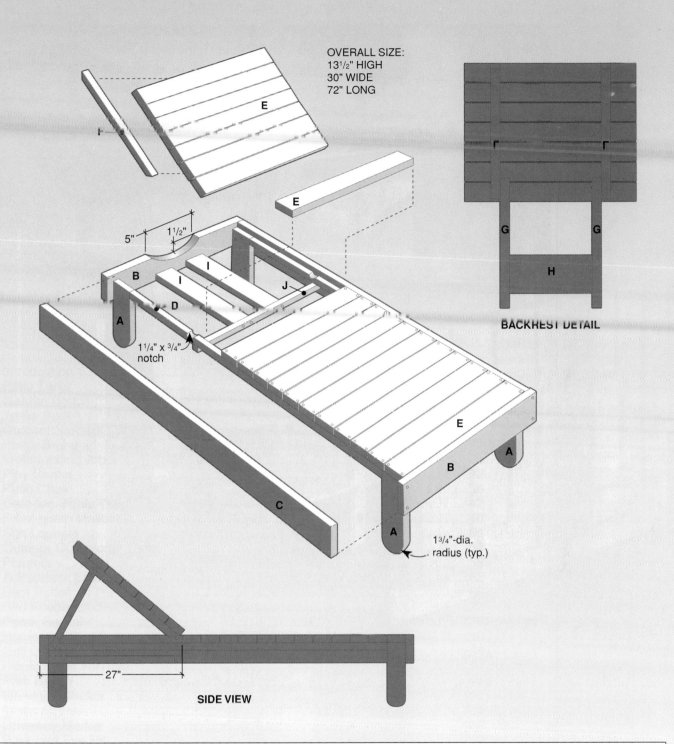

OVERALL SIZE:
13½" HIGH
30" WIDE
72" LONG

5" 1½"

1¼" × ¾"
notch

1¾"-dia.
radius (typ.)

BACKREST DETAIL

27"

SIDE VIEW

Cutting List				
Key	Part	Dimension	Pcs.	Material
A	Leg	1½ × 3½ × 12"	4	Pine
B	Frame end	1½ × 5½ × 30"	2	Pine
C	Frame side	1½ × 5½ × 69"	2	Pine
D	Ledger	1½ × 1½ × 62"	2	Pine
E	Slat	1½ × 3½ × 27"	19	Pine

Cutting List				
Key	Part	Dimension	Pcs.	Material
F	Back brace	1½ × 1½ × 22"	2	Pine
G	Back support	1½ × 1½ × 20"	2	Pine
H	Cross brace	1½ × 5½ × 13"	1	Pine
I	Slide support	1½ × 3½ × 24"	2	Pine
J	Slide brace	1½ × 1½ × 27"	1	Pine

Materials: Moisture-resistant wood glue, 2½" deck screws, (2) ¼"-dia. × 3½" carriage bolts with washers and nuts.

Note: Measurements reflect the actual size of dimensional lumber.

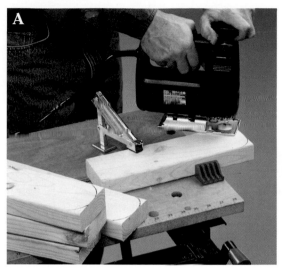

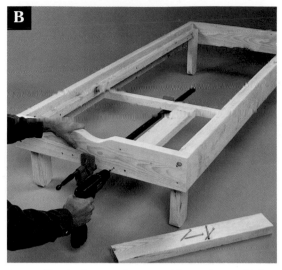

Use a jig saw to cut roundovers on the bottoms of the legs.

Assemble the frame pieces and legs, then add the support boards for the slats and backrest.

Use ⅛"-thick spacers to keep an even gap between slats as you fasten them to the back braces and the ledgers in the bed frame.

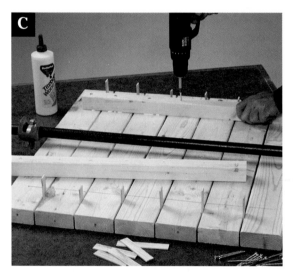

Directions: Sun Lounger

MAKE THE LEGS. Start by cutting the legs (A) to length from 2 × 4 pine. To ensure uniform length, cut four 2 × 4s to about 13" in length, then clamp them together edge to edge and gang-cut them to final length

(12") with a circular saw. Use a compass to scribe a 3½"-radius roundoff cut at the bottom corners of each leg. Make the roundoff cuts with a jig saw **(photo A),** then sand smooth. The rounded leg bottoms help the sun lounger rest firmly on uneven surfaces.

CUT THE FRAME PIECES & LEDGERS. Cut the frame ends (B) and frame sides (C) from 2 × 6 pine. Use a jig saw to cut a 5"-wide, 1½"-deep arc into the top edge of one frame end, centered end to end, to create a handgrip. Cut the ledgers (D) from 2 × 2 pine. Measure 24"

from one end of each ledger and place a mark, then cut a 1¼"-wide, ¾"-deep notch into the top edge of each ledger, centered on the 24" mark. Smooth out the notch with a 1½"-radius drum sander mounted on a power drill (this notch will serve as the pivot for the back support). Sand all parts and smooth out all sharp edges.

ASSEMBLE THE FRAME. The lounge frame consists of the legs, the side and end frame pieces, and the long ledger strips that support the slats. Begin assembly by attaching the frame sides and frame ends to form a box around the legs, with the tops of the frame pieces 1½" above the tops of the legs to leave space for the 2 × 4 slats. Use glue and 2¼" deck screws, driven from the inside of the frame. Attach the ledgers to the frame sides, fitted between the legs, using glue and 2" deck screws. Make sure the ledger tops are flush with the tops of the legs, and the notches are at the same end as the notch in the frame.

TIP

For a better appearance, always keep the screws aligned. In some cases, you may want to add some screws for purely decorative purposes: in this project, we drove 1" deck screws into the backrest slats to continue the lines created by the screw heads in the lower lounge slats.

CUT & INSTALL THE BACKREST SUPPORTS. Cut the slide brace (J) from 2 × 2 pine. Position the slide brace between the frame sides, 24" from the notched frame end, fitted against the bottom edges of the ledgers. Glue and screw the slide brace to the bottom edges of the ledgers. Cut the slide supports (I) to length from 2 × 4 pine, then position the supports so they are about 3" apart, centered below the notch in the frame end. The ends of the supports should fit neatly against the frame end and the slide brace. Attach with glue and screws driven through the frame end and the slide brace, and into the ends of the slide supports **(photo B).**

FASTEN THE SLATS. Start by cutting all the slats (E) for the project to length from 2 × 4 pine. Use a straightedge guide to ensure straight cuts (the ends will be highly visible), or simply hold a speed square against the edges of the boards and run your circular saw along the edge of the speed square. Cut the back braces (F) from 2 × 2 pine. Lay seven of the slats on a flat worksurface, and slip ⅛"-wide spacers between the slats. With the ends of the slats flush, set the back braces onto the faces of the slats, 4" in from the ends. Drive a 2" deck screw through the brace and into each slat **(photo C).** Install the remaining slats in the bed frame, spaced ⅛" apart, by driving two screws through each slat end and into the tops of the ledgers. One end slat should be ⅛" from the inside of the uncut frame end, and the other 27" from the outside of the notched frame end.

ASSEMBLE THE BACKREST SUPPORT FRAMEWORK. The adjustable backrest is held in place by a small framework that is attached to the back braces. The framework can either be laid flat so the backrest also lies flat, or raised up and fitted against the inside of the notched frame end to support the backrest in an upright position. Cut the back supports (G) from 2 × 2 pine, then clamp the pieces together face to face, with the ends flush. Clamp a belt sander to your worksurface, and use it as a grinder to round off the supports on one end. Cut the cross brace (H) to length from 2 × 6 pine. Position the cross brace between the back supports, 2" from the non-rounded ends, and attach with glue and 2½" deck screws driven through the cross brace and into the edges of the supports. Next, position the rounded ends of the supports so they fit between the ends of the back braces, overlapping by 2½" when laid flat. Drill a ¼"-dia. guide hole through the braces and the supports at each overlap joint. Thread ¼"-dia. × 3"-long carriage bolts through the guide holes, with a flat washer between each support and brace. Hand-tighten a washer and nylon locking nut onto each bolt end (see **photo D** for a view of how these parts fit together).

INSTALL THE BACKREST. Set the backrest onto the ledger boards near the notched end of the frame. With the backrest raised, tighten the locking nut on the backrest support framework until it is tight enough to hold the framework together securely, while still allowing the joint to pivot **(photo D).**

APPLY THE FINISHING TOUCHES. Sand all surfaces and edges **(photo E)** to eliminate the possibility of slivers. After sanding, we applied two coats of water-based, exterior polyurethane for a smooth, protective finish. You may prefer to use light-colored exterior paint.

D

Use a washer and nylon locking nut to fasten the back braces to the back supports.

E

Sand all surfaces carefully to eliminate splinters, and check to make sure all screw heads are set below the wood surface.

Outdoor Occasional Table

The traditional design of this deck table provides a stylishly simple addition to any porch, deck or patio.

CONSTRUCTION MATERIALS	
Quantity	**Lumber**
2	1 × 3" × 8' cedar
6	1 × 4" × 8' cedar

Create a functional yet stylish accent to your porch, deck or patio with this cedar deck table. This table makes an ideal surface for serving cold lemonade on hot summer days, a handy place to set your plate during a family cookout, or simply a comfortable place to rest your feet after a long day. Don't be fooled by its lightweight design and streamlined features; this little table is extremely sturdy. Structural features such as middle and end stringers tie the aprons and legs together and transfer weight from the table slats to the legs. This attractive little table is easy to build and will provide many years of durable service.

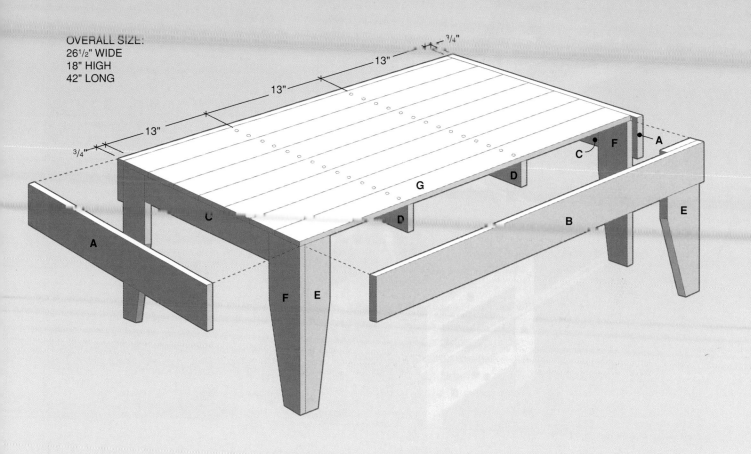

OVERALL SIZE:
26½" WIDE
18" HIGH
42" LONG

13"

13"

13"

13"

¾"

¾"

A

F

C

D

G

D

C

B

A

E

E

F

E

F

	Cutting List						Cutting List			
Key	**Part**	**Dimension**	**Pcs.**	**Material**		**Key**	**Part**	**Dimension**	**Pcs.**	**Material**
A	End apron	¾ × 3½ × 26½"	2	Cedar		**E**	Narrow leg side	¾ × 2½ × 17¼"	4	Cedar
B	Side apron	¾ × 3½ × 40½"	2	Cedar		**F**	Wide leg side	¾ × 3½ × 17¼"	4	Cedar
C	End stringer	¾ × 2½ × 18"	2	Cedar		**G**	Slat	¾ × 3½ × 40½"	7	Cedar
D	Middle stringer	¾ × 2½ × 25"	2	Cedar						

Materials: Moisture-resistant glue, 1¼" deck screws.

Note: Measurements reflect the actual size of dimensional lumber.

Use a speed square as a cutting guide and gang-cut the table parts when possible for uniform results.

Mark the ends of the tapers on the leg sides, then connect the marks to make taper cutting lines.

Directions: Outdoor Occasional Table

MAKE THE STRINGERS & APRONS. The stringers and aprons form a frame for the tabletop slats. To make them, cut the end aprons (A) and side aprons (B) from 1 × 4 cedar **(photo A).** For fast, straight cutting, use a speed square as a saw guide—the flange on the speed square hooks over the edge of the boards to hold it securely in place while you cut. Cut the end stringers (C) and middle stringers (D) from 1 × 3 cedar.

MAKE THE LEG PARTS. Cut the narrow leg sides (E) to length from 1 × 3 cedar. Cut the wide leg sides (F) to length from 1 × 4 cedar. On one wide leg side piece, measure 8¾" along one edge of leg side and place a mark. Measure across the bottom end of the leg side 1½" and place a

TIP

Rip-cut cedar 1 × 4s to 2½" in width if you are unable to find good clear cedar 1 × 3s (nominal). When rip-cutting, always use a straightedge guide for your circular saw. A straight piece of lumber clamped to your workpiece makes an adequate guide, or buy a metal straightedge guide with built-in clamps.

Use a jig saw or circular saw to cut the leg tapers.

mark. Connect the two marks to create a cutting line for the leg taper. Mark cutting lines for the tapers on all four wide leg sides **(photo B).** On the thin leg sides, measure 8¾" along an edge and ¾" across the bottom end to make endpoints for the taper cutting lines. Clamp each leg side to your worksurface, and cut along the taper cutoff line, using a jig saw or circular saw, to create the tapered leg sides **(photo C).** Sand all of the leg parts until smooth.

ASSEMBLE THE LEG PAIRS. Apply a ½"-wide layer of moisture-resistant glue on the face of a wide leg side, next to the untapered edge. Then apply a thin layer of glue to the untapered edge of a narrow leg side. Join the leg sides together at a right angle to form a leg pair. Reinforce the joint with 1¼" deck screws. Glue and screw the rest of the leg pairs in the same manner **(photo D).** Be careful not to use too much glue: it can get messy and also will cause problems later if you

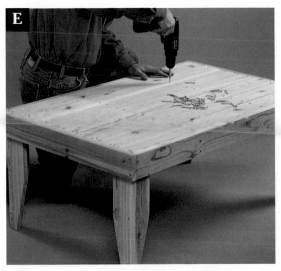

Fasten the leg pairs by driving deck screws through the face of the wide side and into the narrow edge.

Test the layout of the slats before you fasten them, adjusting as necessary to make sure gaps are even.

plan to stain or clear-coat the finish.

MAKE THE TABLETOP FRAME. Now fasten the side aprons (B) to the leg pairs with glue and screws. Be sure to screw from the back side of the leg pair and into the side aprons so the screw heads will be concealed. The narrow leg side of each pair should be facing in toward the center of the side apron, with the outside faces of the wide leg sides flush with the ends of the side apron. The tops of the leg pairs should be ¾" down from the tops of the side aprons to create recesses for the tabletop slats. Now attach the end aprons (A) to the leg assemblies. Use glue, and drive screws from the back side of the leg pairs. Make sure the end aprons are positioned so the ends are flush with the outside faces of the side aprons. Once the aprons are fastened to the pairs, attach the end stringers (C) to the end aprons between the leg pairs. Use glue, and drive the screws from the back sides of the end stringers

and into the end aprons. Cut the middle stringers (D) to length, then measure 13" in from the inside face of each end stringer and mark reference lines on the side aprons for positioning the middle stringers (see page 55). Attach the middle stringers to the side aprons, centered on the reference lines, using glue and deck screws driven through the side aprons and into the ends of the middle stringers. Make sure the middle stringers are positioned ¾" down from the tops of the side aprons.

CUT AND INSTALL THE SLATS. Before you start cutting the slats (G), measure the inside dimension between the end aprons to be sure that the slat length is correct. Once you've confirmed the length, cut the slats to length from 1 × 4 cedar, using a circular saw and a speed square to keep the cuts square. It is extremely important to make square cuts on the ends of the slats because they are going to be the most visible cuts on the entire table. Once all the slats are cut, run a bead of glue along the top faces of

the middle and end stringers. Screw the slats to the stringers leaving a gap of approximately ⅟₁₆" between each of the individual slats **(photo E)**.

APPLY THE FINISHING TOUCHES. Smooth all sharp edges by using a router with a roundover bit or a power sander with medium-grit (#100 to 120) sandpaper. Finish-sand the entire table, clean off the sanding residue and apply your finish. We used clear wood sealer. We left the screw heads exposed, but if you prefer, you can fill the screw counterbores with tinted wood putty.

> TIP
>
> *Clamp all workpiece parts whenever possible during the assembly process. Clamping will hold glued-up and squared-up parts securely in place until you permanently fasten them with screws. Large, awkward assemblies will be more manageable with the help of a few clamps.*

Planters

*These cedar planters are simple projects that can transform a plain
plant container into an attractive outdoor accessory.*

Construction Materials	
Quantity	**Lumber**
1	1 × 10" × 6' cedar
1	¼ × 20 × 20" hardboard or plywood

Add a decorative touch
to your deck, porch or
patio with these stylish
cedar planters. Created using
square pieces of cedar fashioned together in different
design patterns, the styles
shown above feature circular
cutouts that are sized to hold a
standard 24-ounce coffee can.
To build them, simply cut 1 × 10
cedar to 9¼" lengths, then
make 7¼"-diameter cutouts in
the components as necessary.
We used a router and template
to make the cutouts with production speed. Follow the assembly instructions (see page
61 and the diagrams on page
59) to create the three designs
above. Or, you can create your
own designs by rearranging
the components or altering the
cutout size.

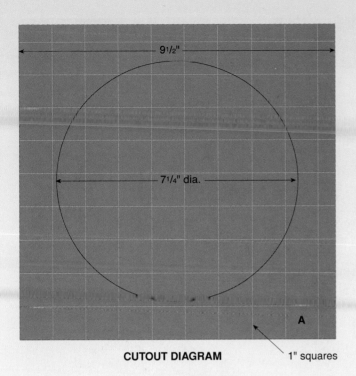

9½"

7¼" dia.

A

CUTOUT DIAGRAM

1" squares

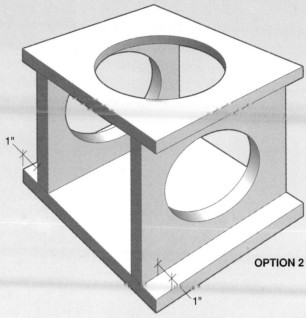

1"

1"

OPTION 2

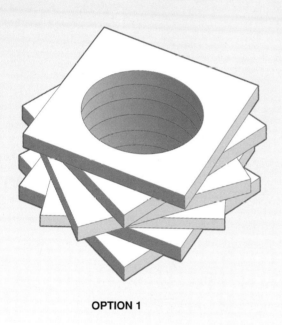

OPTION 1

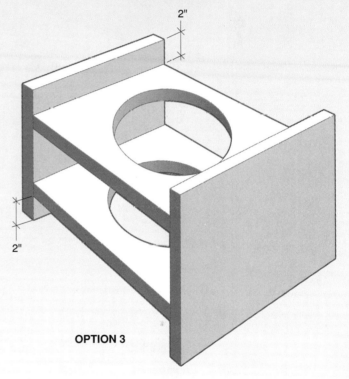

2"

2"

OPTION 3

Cutting List				
Key	**Part**	**Dimension**	**Pcs.**	**Material**
A	Component	¾ × 9¼ × 9¼"	*	Cedar

Materials: Moisture-resistant glue, 2" deck screws, 24-ounce coffee can, finishing materials.

* Number of pieces varies according to planter style.

Note: Measurements reflect the actual size of dimensional lumber.

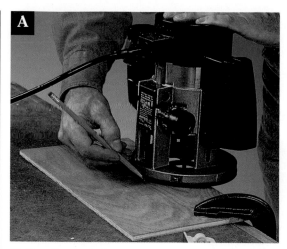

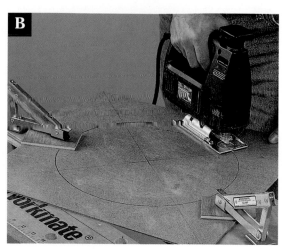

Outline the router base onto scrap material to help determine the router-base radius.

Cut out the router template using a jig saw.

Drill a starter hole for the router bit in the centers of the components.

Directions: Planters

MAKE THE ROUTER TEMPLATE. Using a router and a router template is an excellent method for doing production style work with uniform results. To create the cutout components for our planters, we made a circular template to use as a cutting guide for the router. Determining the size of the template circle is simple: just add the radius of your router base to the radius of your fin-ished cutout (3⅝" in the project as shown). Begin by finding the radius of your router base: first, install a 1"-long straight bit in your router (for fast cutting, use a ¾"-diameter bit, but make sure you use the same bit for making the template and cut-ting the components); make a shallow cut into the edge of a piece of scrap wood; then, with the router bit stopped, trace around the outside edge of the router base with a pencil **(photo A).** Measure from the perimeter of the router cut to the router-base outline to find the radius. Add 3⅝" for the ra-dius of a 24-ounce coffee can and, using a compass, draw a circle with this measurement onto the template material. Cut out the router template using a jig saw **(photo B).**

MAKE THE PARTS. The planters are built from identical compo-nents (A) of 1 × 10 cedar. Cut the number of components re-quired for your design to length, then make circular cutouts on those components that require them. To make a circular cutout, start by draw-ing diagonal lines connecting the corners of the component. The point of intersection is the center of the square board. Center the template on the component, and clamp it in place. Use a drill to bore a 1"-diameter starter hole for the router bit (unless you are using a plunge router—see *Tip,* left) at the center **(photo C).** Posi-tion the router bit inside the hole. Turn the router on and move it away from the starter hole until the router base con-tacts the template. Pull the router in a counterclockwise direction around the inside of the template to make the cutout. Smooth any sharp edges with sandpaper.

OPTION 1

Option 1. *Attach the pieces on the stacked planter from top to bottom, ending with a solid base. To make this stacked planter, you need six pieces of 1 × 10 cedar. Cut them to length, and rout circular shapes in five of them. The solid piece will be the base. Stack the pieces on top of the base component. Place a painted coffee can in the center and arrange the sections to achieve a spiralling effect (see* Diagram, page 59). *Use a pencil to mark the locations of the pieces. Remove the can and fasten the pieces together using glue and deck screws. Attach the pieces by driving the deck screws through the lower pieces into the upper pieces, fastening the base last.*

OPTION 2

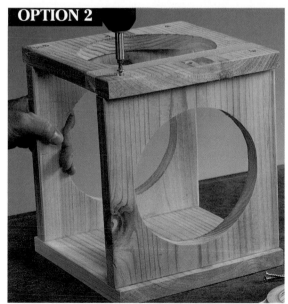

Option 2. *Use four components on this option to create a planter with three cutout components and a solid base. Measure and mark lines 1" from each side edge on the solid component and one of the cut-out components. Attach the inner components with their inside faces flush with these lines. Fasten the solid component to the sides with moisture-resistant glue and deck screws, then attach the remaining cut-out component to finish the planter. Insert a painted coffee can.*

OPTION 3

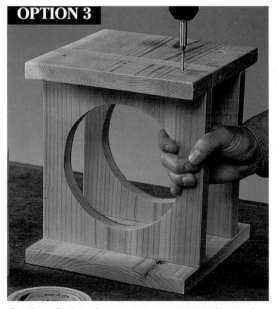

Option 3. *Attach two components with circular cutouts to the inside faces of two solid components to make this planter. Measure and mark guidelines 2" from the top and bottom edges on the two solid components. Fasten the two cut-out components between the others with moisture-resistant glue and deck screws, making sure their outside edges are flush with the drawn guidelines. Insert a painted coffee can.*

Adirondack Chair

PROJECT
POWER TOOLS

You will find dozens of patterns and plans for building popular Adirondack chairs in just about any bookstore, but few are simpler to make than this clever project.

Adirondack furniture has become a standard on decks, porches and patios throughout the world. It's no mystery why this distinctive furniture style has become so popular. The straightforward design, expansive surfaces, and the unmatched stability are just a few of the reasons, and our Adirondack chair offers all of these benefits, and more. But unlike most of the Adirondack chairs you may find, this chair is also very easy to build. There are no complex compound angles to cut, no intricate details on the back and seat slats, and no mortise-and-tenon joints. Like all projects in this book, our Adirondack chair can be built by any do-it-yourselfer, using basic tools and simple techniques. But because this design features all the elements that make an Adirondack chair an Adirondack chair, your guests and neighbors may never guess that you built it yourself.

We made our Adirondack chair out of cedar and finished it with clear wood sealer. But you may prefer to build your version from pine (a traditional wood type for Adirondack furniture), especially if you plan to paint the chair. White, battleship gray and forest green are common colors for Adirondack furniture. Be sure to use quality exterior paint with a glossy or enamel finish.

CONSTRUCTION MATERIALS

Quantity	Lumber
1	2 × 6" × 8' cedar
1	2 × 4" × 10' cedar
1	1 × 6" × 14' cedar
1	1 × 4" × 12' cedar
1	1 × 2" × 8' cedar

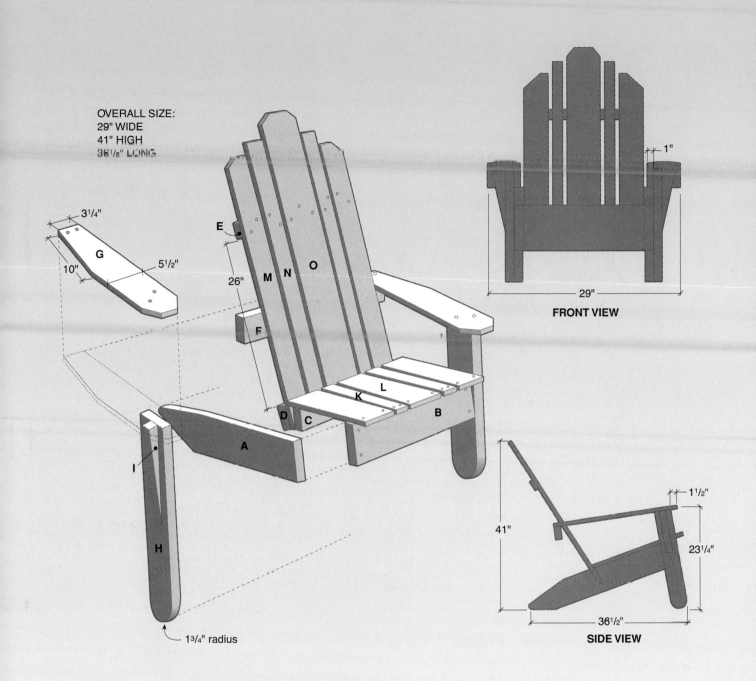

OVERALL SIZE:
29" WIDE
41" HIGH
36½" LONG

3¼"

G

10"

5½"

FRONT VIEW

29"

1"

E

26"

M N O

F

D C

K L

B

A

I

H

1¾" radius

41"

36½"

1½"

23¼"

SIDE VIEW

Cutting List				
Key	**Part**	**Dimension**	**Pcs.**	**Material**
A	Leg	1½ × 5½ × 34½"	2	Cedar
B	Front	1½ × 5½ × 21"	1	Cedar
C	Seat support	1½ × 3½ × 18"	1	Cedar
D	Low back brace	1½ × 3½ × 18"	1	Cedar
E	High back brace	¾ × 3½ × 18"	1	Cedar
F	Arm cleat	1½ × 3½ × 24"	1	Cedar
G	Arm	¾ × 5½ × 28"	2	Cedar
H	Post	1½ × 3½ × 22"	2	Cedar

Cutting List				
Key	**Part**	**Dimension**	**Pcs.**	**Material**
I	Arm brace	1½ × 2¼ × 10"	2	Cedar
K	Narrow seat slat	¾ × 1½ × 20"	2	Cedar
L	Center seat slat	¾ × 5½ × 20"	3	Cedar
M	End back slat	¾ × 3½ × 36"	2	Cedar
N	Narrow back slat	¾ × 1½ × 38"	2	Cedar
O	Center back slat	¾ × 5½ × 40"	1	Cedar

Materials: Moisture-resistant glue, deck screws (1¼", 1½", 2", 3"), ⅜ × 2½" lag screws with washers, finishing materials.

Note: Measurements reflect the actual size of dimensional lumber.

Cut tapers into the back edges of the legs.

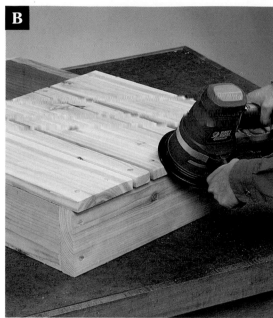

Round over the sharp slat edges with a router or power sander.

Directions:
Adirondack Chair

CUT THE LEGS. Wide, sprawling back legs that support the seat slats and stretch to the ground on a near-horizontal plane are telltale features of Adirondack style. To make the legs (A), first cut two 34½"-long pieces of 2 × 6. Mark the tapers onto the back end of one board. First, mark a point on the end of the board, 2" from the edge. Then mark another point on the edge, 6" from the end. Connect the points with a straightedge. Then, mark another point on the same end, 2¼" in from the other edge. Mark a point on that edge, 10" from the end. Connect these points to make a cutting line for the other taper. Make the two taper cuts with a circular saw, then use the leg as a template for marking identical tapers on the other leg board. Cut the second leg **(photo A).**

Make decorative cuts on the fronts of the arms (shown) and the tops of the back slats, using a jig saw.

BUILD THE SEAT. The legs form the sides of the box frame that supports the seat slats. Cut the front apron (B) and seat support (C) to size. Attach the apron to the front ends of the legs with glue and 3" deck screws driven through counterbored pilot holes. For the 3" deck screws used throughout most of this project, drill ⅛"-dia. pilot holes through ⅜"-dia. × ¼"-deep counterbores, then insert ⅜"-dia. cedar plugs into the counterbores when assembly is finished. Position the seat support so the inside face is 16½" from the inside edge of the front apron. Attach the seat support between the legs, making sure the tops of the part are flush.

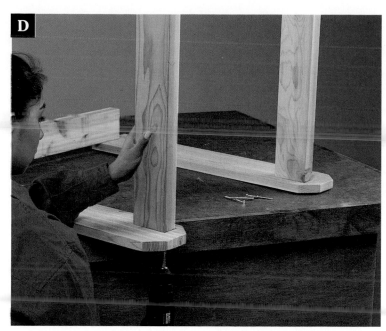

D

Attach the square ends of the posts to the undersides of the arms, being careful to position the part correctly.

Next, cut the seat slats (K) and (L) to length from 1 × 2 and 1 × 6, respectively, and sand the ends smooth. Arrange the slats on top of the seat box (see page 65), with ⅜" spaces between slats—use wood scraps as spacers. The slats should overhang the front of the seat box by ¾". Fasten the seat slats by driving counterbored 2" deck screws through the ends of the slats and into the top of the front apron and the seat support in back. Be careful to keep the counterbores aligned so the cedar plugs form straight lines across the front and back of the seat. Once all the slats are installed, use a router with a ¼" roundover bit (or a power sander) to smooth the edges and ends of the slats **(photo B).**

MAKE THE BACK SLATS. Like the seat slats, the back slats in our design are made from three sizes of dimension lumber (1 × 4, 1 × 2, and 1 × 6). Cut the back slats (M), (N), (O), to size. For a decorative touch

that is simple to create, we trimmed off corners on the wider slats. On the 1 × 6 slat (O), mark points 1" in from the outside, top corners of the slat, then mark points on the outside edges, 1" down from the corners. Connect the points, then trim off the corners with a jig saw, following the lines. Mark the 1 × 4 slats 2" from one top corner, in both directions. Draw cutting lines, then trim off these corners.

ATTACH BACK SLATS TO BRACE. Cut the low back brace (D) and high back brace (E). Set the braces on a flat worksurface, then slip ¾"-thick spacers under the high brace so the top is level with the low brace. Arrange the back slats on top of the braces with

the same pattern and spacing used with the seat slats. The untrimmed ends of the slats should be flush with the bottom edge of the low back brace, and the bottom of the high back brace should be 26" above the top of the low brace. Use ¾" spacers to set gaps and make sure the braces are exactly perpendicular to the slats. Attach the slats to the low brace with counterbored 2" deck screws, and to the high brace with 1¼" deck screws (see page 65 for a suggested screw pattern).

CUT THE ARMS. The broad arms of this Adirondack chair are supported by posts in front, and a cleat that is attached to the backs of the chair slats. Start by cutting the arms (G) to size. For decoration, cut a triangle with 1½"-long sides from the front corners of each arm, using a jig saw or circular saw **(photo C).** Then, make a tapered cut on the inside, back edge of each arm. Mark points for the cut onto the back end of each arm, 3¼" in from each inside edge. Mark the outside edges 10" from the back, connect the points, then cut the tapers with a circular saw or jig saw. Sand all edges smooth.

ORIGINS OF THE ADIRONDACK STYLE

The Adirondack style originated in Westport, New York, around the turn of the century, when the "Westport chair" made its first appearance. It was very similar to the modern Adirondack chair, except that the back and seat were usually made from single pieces of very wide and clear hemlock or basswood. These chairs became very popular along the East Coast, with many different models cropping up. Because of deforestation, however, the wide boards in the Westport-style furniture became hard to obtain. So designers came up with versions of the chair that featured narrower back and seat slats, and the prototype for the Adirondack chair, as we know it today, was born.

Drive screws through each post and into the top of an arm brace to stabilize the arm/post joint.

Clamp wood braces to the parts of the chair to hold them in position while you fasten the parts together.

ASSEMBLE THE ARMS, CLEATS & POSTS. Cut the arm cleat (F) and make a mark 2½" in from each end. Set the cleat on edge on your worksurface. Position the arms on the top edge of the cleat so the back ends of the arms are flush with the back of the cleat and the untapered edge of each arm is aligned with the 2½" mark. Fasten the arms to the cleats using glue and counterbored 3" deck screws. Cut the posts (H) to size, then use a compass to mark a 1¾" radius roundover cut on each bottom post cor-

TIP

Making tapered cuts with a circular is not difficult if the alignment marks on your saw base are accurate. Before attempting to make a tapered cut where you enter the wood at an angle, always make test cuts on scrap wood to be sure the blade starts cutting in alignment with the alignment marks on your saw. If not, either re-set your alignment marks, or compensate for the difference when you cut the tapers.

ner (the rounded bottoms make the Adirondack chair more stable on uneven surfaces). Position the arms on top of the square ends of the posts, with the faces of the post parallel to the sides of the arms. The posts should be set back 1½" from the front ends of the arm, and 1" from the inside edge of the arm. Fasten the arms to the posts with glue and counterbored 3" deck screws **(photo D).** Cut tapered arm braces (I) from wood scraps, making sure the grain of the wood runs lengthwise (see page 65). Position an arm brace at the outside of each arm/post joint, centered side to side on the post. Attach each brace with glue and 2" counterbored deck screws driven through the inside face of the

post and into the brace, near the top **(photo E).** Also drive a 2" deck screw down through each arm and into the top of the brace.

ASSEMBLE THE CHAIR. All that remains is to join the back, seat/leg assembly and arm/post assembly to complete the construction of the Adirondack chair. Before you start, gather up some scrap pieces of wood to use to help brace the parts while you fasten them together. First, set the seat/leg assembly onto your worksurface, clamping a piece of scrap wood to the front apron to raise the front of the assembly until the bottoms of the legs are flush on the surface (about 10"). Use a similar technique to brace the arm/post assembly so the bottom of the back cleat is 20" above the worksurface. Arrange the arm/post assembly so the posts fit around the front

66

of the seat/leg assembly, with the bottom edge of the apron flush with the front edges of the posts. Drill a ¼"-dia. pilot hole through the inside of each leg and partway into the post. Drive a ⅜ × 2½"-long lag screw (with washer) through each pilot hole, but do not tighten completely in case you need to make any assembly adjustments **(photo F)**. Remove the braces. Now, slide the back into position so the low back brace is between the legs, and the slats are resting against the front of the arm cleat. Clamp the back to the seat support with a C-clamp, making sure the top of the low brace is flush with the tops of the legs where they meet. Use a square to check to see that the ends of the seat slats meet the front faces of the back slats at a right angle. If not, adjust the relative position of the assemblies until a right angle is achieved. Fully tighten the lag screws at the post/leg joints, then add a second lag screw at each joint. Finally, drive three evenly spaced 1½" deck screws through counterbored pilot holes (near the top edge of the arm cleat) and into the back slats to secure the back **(photo G)**. Also drive 3" screws through the legs and into the ends of the lower back brace.

APPLY FINISHING TOUCHES. Glue ¼"-thick, ⅜"-dia. cedar wood plugs into all the visible screw counterbores **(photo H)**. After the glue dries, sand the plugs level with the surrounding surface, then finish-sand all the exposed surfaces with 120-grit sandpaper. Finish as desired—we simply applied a coat of clear wood sealer.

Drive screws through the arm cleat, near the top and into the slats.

Glue cedar plugs into counterbores to conceal the screw holes.

Boot Butler

*A traditional piece of home furniture, the boot butler combines
shoe storage and seating in one dependable unit.*

CONSTRUCTION MATERIALS

Quantity	Lumber
1	¾" × 4 × 8' plywood
2	4" × 4' pine ranch molding

Our boot butler was designed for an enclosed front porch, but it can be used near any household entrance. It provides plenty of storage space and gives you a solid seat when you're putting on or removing your shoes and boots. This boot butler is a classic piece of household furniture that we modernized and simplified for your home. Just fit some plastic boot trays neatly onto the bottom shelf to keep mud from making a filthy mess on the carpet. When the trays get dirty, simply take them out and clean them. The boot butler can handle the footwear of the entire family, and it fits conveniently against the wall to save space and keep unsightly boots and shoes out of busy traffic lanes.

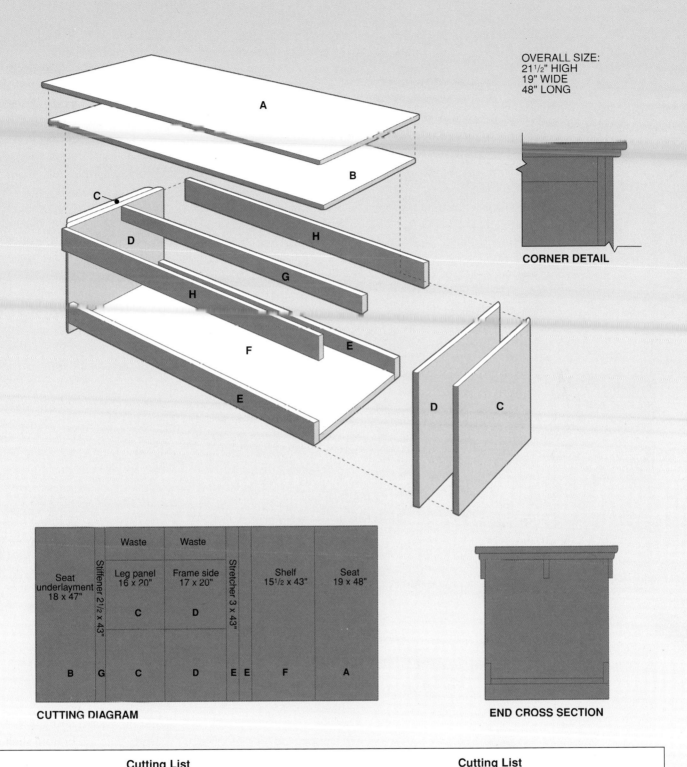

OVERALL SIZE:
21¹/₂" HIGH
19" WIDE
48" LONG

CORNER DETAIL

A

B

C

D

H

G

H

E

F

E

D

C

CUTTING DIAGRAM

Seat
underlayment
18 x 47"

Stiffener 2½ x 43"

Waste

Leg panel
16 x 20"

C

Waste

Frame side
17 x 20"

D

Stretcher 3 x 43"

Shelf
15½ x 43"

Seat
19 x 48"

B G C D E E F A

END CROSS SECTION

Cutting List				
Key	**Part**	**Dimension**	**Pcs.**	**Material**
A	Seat	¾ × 19 × 48"	1	Plywood
B	Underlayment	¾ × 18 × 47"	1	Plywood
C	Leg panel	¾ × 16 × 20"	2	Plywood
D	Frame side	¾ × 17 × 20"	2	Plywood

Cutting List				
Key	**Part**	**Dimension**	**Pcs.**	**Material**
E	Stretcher	¾ × 3 × 43"	2	Plywood
F	Shelf	¾ × 15½ × 43"	1	Plywood
G	Stiffener	¾ × 2½ × 43"	1	Plywood
H	Apron	½ × 3½ × 43¾"	2	Pine

Materials: Moisture-resistant glue, deck screws (1¼", 2"), 8d finish nails, 15 × 21" plastic boot trays, finishing materials.

Note: Measurements reflect the actual size of dimensional lumber.

Directions:
Boot Butler

CUT THE PLYWOOD PARTS. Cut all of the following parts with a circular saw and straightedge (refer to the *Cutting Diagram* on page 09 to see how to lay out and cut all the parts from one sheet of plywood): seat (A), seat underlayment (B), leg panel (C), frame side (D), stretchers (E), shelf (F) and stiffener (G). Smooth out the sides of the legs, the top edges of the stretchers, and all the edges of the seat and underlayment with a sander or a router and ¼" roundover bit.

Use glue to reinforce the joints between the stretchers and the shelf.

ASSEMBLE THE SHELF & STRETCHERS. All the plywood parts are connected with screws and glue. Before you drive the screws, drill counterbores for the screw heads that are just deep enough to be filled with wood filler or putty. Attach the stretchers and shelf by drilling four evenly spaced ³⁄₁₆"-dia. pilot holes through the outside edges of the stretchers and into the front and back edges of the shelf. Keep the screw holes at least 2" from the ends of the stretchers to prevent splitting when you drive the screws. Glue the joints **(photo A),** and drive 2" deck screws through the pilot holes and into the shelf.

BUILD THE BOX FRAME. Now, attach the two frame sides (D) to the ends of the shelf assembly. To accomplish this, mark the location of the parts onto the frame sides. Begin by measuring and marking a line 2" up from the bottom edge of each frame side. This is where the lower edges of the stretchers will fit when the stretchers are installed. The stiffener (G) is positioned between the frame sides, at the top, center points

to provide stability to the box frame. Mark the stiffener position, making sure the top of the stiffener is flush with the tops of the frame sides, and apply glue to all the joints. Clamp the stretchers and stiffener in position with bar clamps. Drill two evenly spaced ³⁄₁₆"-dia. pilot holes through each frame side and into the ends of the stiffener. Drive the 2" deck screws to secure the stiffener **(photo B).** For extra shelf support, drill pilot holes and drive a screw through the center of each frame side into the shelf.

COMPLETE THE LEG ASSEMBLY. Attach leg panels (C) to the outer faces of the frame sides to provide wider, more stable support points for the seat. Put wax paper or newspaper on your work surface to catch any excess glue, then apply glue to the outer face of each frame side, and to the inner face of each leg panel. Press the leg panels against the frame panels, centered side to side to create a ½" reveal on each side of each frame panel. All top and bottom edges should be flush. Clamp each panel pair together **(photo C),** then secure with

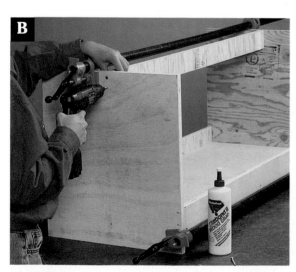

The stiffener is screwed in place between the sides to keep the boot butler square.

A pair of plywood panels are fastened together to create each leg assembly.

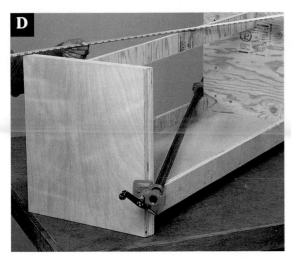

If the frame isn't square, fasten a pipe clamp diagonally across it and tighten.

Set the frame assembly onto the underlayment. Center and trace the outline on the underlayment.

counterbored 1¼" deck screws driven through the frame panels into the leg sides. Check the box frame to make sure it is square by measuring diagonally from corner to corner, across the tops of the leg assembly. Use a pipe clamp to draw the frame together until it is pulled into square, and the diagonal measurements are equal **(photo D).**

ATTACH THE SEAT ASSEMBLY. The seat for the boot butler is made up of two sheets of plywood: a ¾"-thick underlayment (B) layered together with the plywood seat (A). Lay the underlayment on a flat surface, then flip the leg and shelf assembly upside-down and center it on the bottom face of the underlayment. Outline the edges of the frame onto the underlayment for future reference **(photo E).** Flip the leg and shelf assembly upright, and apply glue to the tops of the legs and stiffener. Position the underlayment on the assembly according to the alignment marks. Drill ³⁄₁₆"-dia. counterbored pilot holes through the underlayment into the legs and stiffeners, then

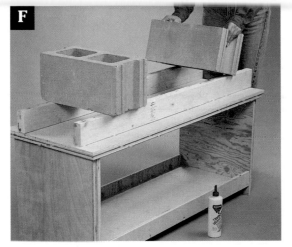

Apply weight on the seat to ensure a solid glue bond with the seat underlayment.

drive 2" deck screws. Apply a thin layer of glue to the top of the underlayment and the underside of the seat. Position the seat onto the underlayment so the overhang is the same on all sides. Set heavy weights on top of the seat to help create a solid glue bond **(photo F).** Drive evenly spaced, counterbored 1¼" deck screws through the underlayment into the seat. Finally, cut the aprons (H) from 4"-wide pine ranch molding. Position the aprons so the tops are flush against the bottom edges of the underlayment, overlapping the edges of the frame panels slightly. Attach with 8d finish nails.

APPLY FINISHING TOUCHES. Fill all of the countersunk screw holes and plywood edges with wood putty and sand smooth. Apply primer and paint—we painted our boot butler with cream-colored exterior latex enamel paint. For a decorative touch, stencil or sponge-paint the surfaces.

> **TIP**
>
> *Rigid, clear plastic boot trays are sold at most discount stores or building centers. The Boot Butler project shown here is designed to hold 15 × 21" plastic boot trays.*

Bird Feeder

*A leftover piece of cedar lap siding is put to good use
in this rustic bird feeder.*

CONSTRUCTION MATERIALS

Quantity	Lumber
1	¾ × 16 × 16" plywood scrap
1	¾" × 6' cedar stop molding
1	8" × 10' cedar lap siding
1	1 × 2" × 8' cedar
1	1"-dia. × 3' dowel

Watching birds feeding in your backyard can be a very relaxing pastime. In this bird feeder project, we used a piece of 8"-wide cedar lap siding to build the decorative feeder box that is mounted on a piece of scrap plywood. The birds didn't seem to mind the leftover building materials, and we were excited because the bird feeder cost almost nothing to build. Even the plastic viewing window covers inside the feeder box were made from a small scrap of clear acrylic left over from another project. To fill this cleverly designed bird feeder, just turn the threaded rod that serves as a hook so it is aligned with the slot in the roof. Then, lift up the roof and add the bird food.

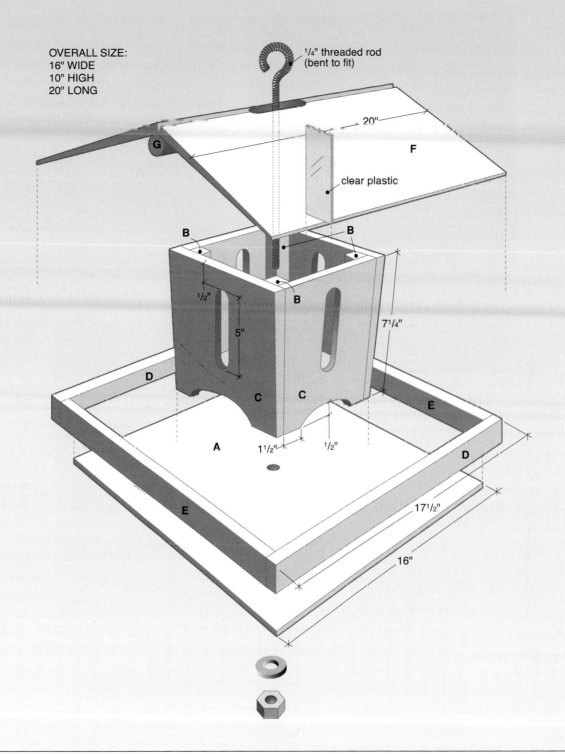

OVERALL SIZE:
16" WIDE
10" HIGH
20" LONG

¼" threaded rod
(bent to fit)

20"

F

clear plastic

G

B

B

B

½"

5"

7¼"

D

C

C

E

A

1½"

½"

D

E

17½"

16"

Cutting List

Key	Part	Dimension	Pcs.	Material
A	Base	¾ × 16 × 16"	1	Plywood
B	Post	¾ × ¾ × 7¼"	4	Cedar
C	Box side	⁵⁄₁₆ × 6 × 7¼"	4	Cedar siding
D	Ledge side	¾ × 1½ × 17½"	2	Cedar

Cutting List

Key	Part	Dimension	Pcs.	Material
E	Ledge end	¾ × 1½ × 16"	2	Cedar
F	Roof panel	⁵⁄₁₆ × 7¼ × 20"	2	Cedar siding
G	Ridge pole	1"-dia. × 20"	1	Dowel

Materials: ¼"-dia. threaded rod with matching nut and washer, wood glue, hotmelt glue, 4d common nails, rigid acrylic or plastic.

Note: Measurements reflect the actual size of dimensional lumber.

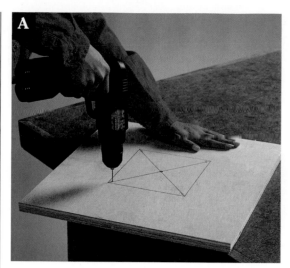

Drill pilot holes at the corners of the feeder box location that is laid out on the plywood base.

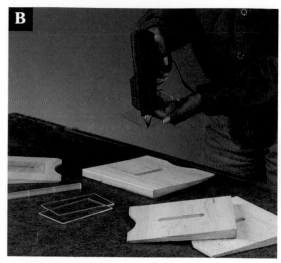

Cover the viewing slots by hot-gluing clear plastic or acrylic pieces to the inside face of each panel.

Directions: Bird Feeder

CUT & PREPARE THE BASE. Cut the plywood base (A) from ¾"-thick plywood. Draw straight diagonal lines from corner to corner to locate the center of the square base. Measure and mark a 6" square in the middle of the base, making sure the lines are parallel to the edges of the base. This square shows the eventual location of the feeder box. Drill a ¼"-dia. hole through the center of the base where the lines cross. Measure in toward the center ⅜" from each corner of the 6" square and mark points. Drill ¹⁄₁₆"-dia. pilot holes all the way through the base at these points **(photo A)**.

PREPARE THE FEEDER BOX PARTS. The posts and box sides form the walls of the feeder box. Vertical grooves in the box sides create viewing windows so you can check the food level. Small arcs cut in the bottoms of the box sides allow the

Mark the profile of the bevel of the siding onto two of the box sides for trimming.

food to flow through to the feeding area in a controlled fashion. To build the feeder box, cut the posts (B) to size from ¾"-square cedar stop molding (if you prefer, you can rip a 3'-long piece of ¾"-thick cedar to ¾" in width to make the posts). From 8" cedar lap siding (actual dimension is 7¼") cut two 6"-wide box sides (C). Then cut two more panels to about 7" in width; these will be trimmed to follow the lap-siding bevels. Now, cut a viewing slot in each box side. First, drill two ½"-dia. starter holes for

a jig saw blade along the center of each box side—make one hole 2" from the top, and the other 2" from the bottom. Connect the starter holes by cutting with a jig saw to cut the slots. Also cut a ½"-deep arc into the bottom of each box side, using the jig saw. Start the cuts 1½" from each end. Smooth out the arcs with a drum sander mounted on a power drill. Finally, cut strips of clear acrylic or plastic slightly larger than the viewing slots. Hot-glue the strips behind the slots on the inside faces of the box sides **(photo B).** To mark cutting lines for trimming two of the

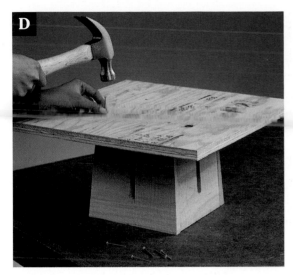

Drive 4d common nails through pilot holes to fasten the feeder box to the base.

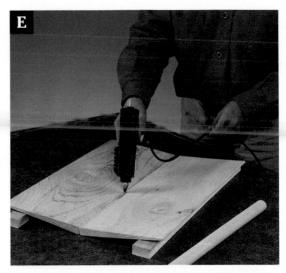

Insert spacers 2" in from the "eaves" of the roof to set the pitch before applying glue to the seam.

box sides to follow the siding bevel, tape the box side together into a box shape. The wide ends of the beveled siding should all be flush. Trace the siding profile onto the the inside faces of the two box ends **(photo C)**. Disassemble the box, then cut along the profile lines with a jig saw.

ASSEMBLE THE FEEDER BOX. Start the assembly by hot-gluing the posts flush with the inside edges on the box sides that are trimmed to follow the bevel profile. Then complete the assembly by hot-gluing the untrimmed box sides to posts.

ATTACH THE BASE. Align the assembled feeder box with the 6" square drawn on the base. Glue the box to the base on these lines, then turn the entire assembly upside down. Attach the base to the feeder box by driving 4d galvanized common nails through the pre-drilled pilot holes in the base, and into the posts on the feeder box **(photo D)**.

INSTALL THE BASE FRAME. Cut the ledge sides (D) and ledge

ends (E) from 1 × 2 cedar, to build a frame around the base so bird food does not spill out. Attach the ledge pieces so the bottoms are flush with the bottom of the base, using hot glue. Reinforce the joint with 4d common nails.

MAKE THE ROOF. Cut the ridge pole (G) from a 1"-dia. dowel, and cut the roof panels (F) from 8" siding. Lay the panels on your worksurface so the wide ends butt together. Slip a 1"-thick spacer 2" in from each of the narrow ends to create the roof pitch. Apply a heavy bead of hot glue into the seam between panels **(photo E)**, then quickly press the ridge pole into the seam before the glue hardens completely. Let the glue harden for at least 15 minutes. Set the roof down (right-side-up) so the ends of the ridge pole each rest on a 2 × 4 block. Drill ⅜"-dia. starter holes through the roof and the ridge pole, 1" on each side of the midpoint of the ridge. Connect the starter holes by cutting with a jig saw. Widen the slot until the ¼"-dia. threaded rod will pass through with only

minimal resistance. Cut the ¼"-dia. threaded rod to 16" in length, then use pliers to bend a 1½"-dia. loop in one end of the rod. Thread the unbent end of the rod through the roof and the hole in the base **(photo F)**, then spin the rod loop so it is perpendicular to the roof ridge (preventing it from slipping into the slot). Tighten a washer and nut onto the end of the rod, loosely enough that the loop can be spun with moderate effort. We didn't apply a finish to our bird feeder.

The bird feeder is held together by a looped, threaded rod that runs through the roof and is secured with a washer and nut on the underside of the base.

Porch Rocker

You don't have to wait until you're retired to enjoy the comfortable embrace of this sturdy plywood and pine porch rocker.

CONSTRUCTION MATERIALS

Quantity	Lumber
1	¾" × 4 × 8' plywood
1	1 × 2" × 3' pine
2	1 × 3" × 8' pine
2	1 × 4" × 10' pine
1	1 × 6" × 4' pine

Escape your daily pressures and problems in this comfortable porch rocker. Our unique design incorporates rocker side panels that are easily cut from plywood sheets with a jig saw. Other frame components consist of solid pine dimensional lumber for simplicity of construction. Broad pine armrests are fitted onto the plywood sides and are big enough to hold a glass of lemonade on those hot summer days. The slatted seat and back provide additional comfort and support while the compact design lets our porch rocker fit nicely even in small porches, where space is at a premium.

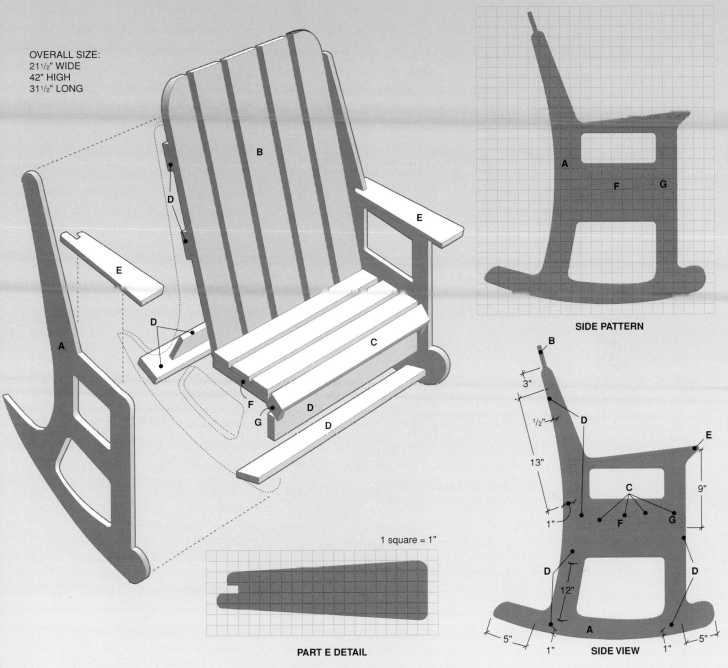

OVERALL SIZE:
21½" WIDE
42" HIGH
31½" LONG

1 square = 1½"

SIDE PATTERN

1 square = 1"

PART E DETAIL

SIDE VIEW

Cutting List				
Key	**Part**	**Dimension**	**Pcs.**	**Material**
A	Sides	¾ × 32 × 39¾"	2	Plywood
B	Back slat	¾ × 3½ × 28"	5	Pine
C	Seat slat	¾ × 3½ × 20"	4	Pine
D	Stretcher	¾ × 2½ × 20"	6	Pine

Cutting List				
Key	**Part**	**Dimension**	**Pcs.**	**Material**
E	Arm	¾ × 5½ × 20"	2	Pine
F	Seat cleat	¾ × 1½ × 8"	2	Pine
G	Front seat cleat	¾ × 1½ × 3"	2	Pine

Materials: Moisture resistant glue, wood screws (#8 × 1¼", #8 × 1½"), finishing materials.

Note: Measurements reflect the actual size of dimensional lumber.

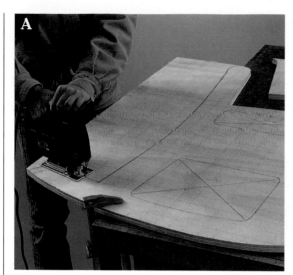

Cut out the rocker sides from 48 × 48" pieces of plywood using a jig saw.

Cut the curved contours at the tops of the outer back slats using a jig saw.

Directions: Porch Rocker

CREATE THE PLYWOOD SIDES. The sides are cut from 48 × 48" pieces of ¾"-thick plywood. Start by using the porch rocker detail drawing (page 77) to lay out the rocker sides on ¾" plywood. Lay out the side pattern on a 48 × 48" piece of plywood. Make marks at 1½" intervals along all sides, then connect the marks to create a layout grid. Use the side pattern (page 77) as a reference for drawing the side shape onto the plywood. Once the sides are laid out and marked, cut out the rocker sides using a jig saw **(photo A).** For interior cutouts, drill out the corners with a ⅜" bit, then use a jig saw to connect the holes by cutting along the layout lines. Lay the side on another 48 × 48" piece of plywood, trace the design and proceed to cut out the other side. Use a router with a

Clamp the workpiece securely to the workbench when using a router. Align the cutting guide and clamp it in place.

¼" roundover bit or a palm sander to smooth all of the edges, except those edges where the arms will be attached.

CUT THE SLATS, CLEATS AND STRETCHERS. The slats, cleats and stretchers are very simple to make. Start by cutting the back slats (B) to length from 1 × 4 lumber. Lay out a 3"-radius contour on the top ends of the two outside slats using a compass or by simply tracing an appropriately-sized tin can, then cut the curved

contours with a jig saw **(photo B).** Smooth out the jig saw cuts with a belt sander or a drum sander attachment on a drill. Next, cut the seat slats (C) to length from 1 × 4 lumber and the stretchers (D) to length from 1 × 3 lumber. Then cut the seat cleats (F) and (G) to length from 1 × 2 lumber.

MAKE THE ARMS. Making the arms involves cutting tapers and radius corners, and also requires you to cut a groove with

TIP

When using a grid-type pattern, enlarge the pattern on a photocopier so it is as close to actual size as possible to make it easier to transfer to the cutting stock.

a router. Start by cutting two 24"-long pieces of 1 × 6 lumber. Lay out the arms on each piece according to the arm detail diagram (page 77). Then, clamp the pieces to your workbench and, using a router with a straightedge cutting guide and a ¾" straight bit, start at one end and cut a ⅜"-deep, ¾"-wide groove down the center of each arm **(photo C).** Stop the groove cut 1½" from the front edge of the arm, otherwise the groove will be visible from the front of the rocker. Next, cut out the arms along the layout lines. Cut the curved corners with a jig saw and the tapers using a jig saw or circular saw. With a router and a ¼" round-over bit, smooth all of the edges on the arms. Sand all of the edges and surfaces before assembly.

ASSEMBLE THE PORCH ROCKER. The assembly is fairly quick and easy. On the inside surfaces of the plywood sides, lay out the locations of all stretchers according to the detail diagram. Drill pilot holes from the inside out, then on the outside surface, counterbore the pilot holes **(photo D).** Fill the screw holes with wood filler when assembly is complete. Next, lay out the locations for the seat cleats, then glue and screw them in place using #8 × 1¼" wood screws. Drive the screws through the cleats into the rocker sides. Attach the stretchers, using glue and screws, in the designated locations on both rocker sides. Start with the four corner stretchers, then the two remaining stretchers. Attach the seat slats to the seat cleats using glue and wood

screws, again slightly counter-sinking the screws so the holes can be filled with wood filler. Complete the assembly process by attaching the back slats to the stretchers and to the rear seat slats using glue and screws **(photo E).** Use ⅜"-thick pieces of scrap wood for spacers between the slats to keep them properly aligned during the assembly process.

APPLY THE FINISHING TOUCHES. Fill all open screw holes and voids in the plywood using a quality wood filler. Finish-sand the surfaces and edges of the rocker by hand or with a palm

sander, generally up to 150-grit. Be sure to use a quality primer and then a quality enamel paint, designed for exterior use and greater durability. Choose a light color to reduce the heat absorption from direct sunlight.

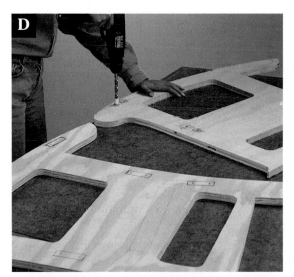

Drill pilot holes to fasten the stretchers to the sides. Counterbore the holes to recess the screw heads.

Fasten the back slats to the stretchers. Use spacers to hold the slats in position during fastening

Hammock Stand

Now you can enjoy the unique pleasure of napping in your own hammock—even if there isn't a tree or fence post in sight.

CONSTRUCTION MATERIALS	
Quantity	**Lumber**
3	1 × 8" × 10' pine
1	1 × 8" × 8' pine
6	1 × 10" × 8' pine
1	2 × 4" × 8' pine
2	2 × 8" × 8' pine

For everyone who has longed for the pleasure of having a backyard hammock, but has lacked a good spot to hang one, this hammock stand is a dream come true. With this Adirondack-inspired structure proudly stationed on your patio or deck, you'll be well on your way to forgetting your day-to-day pressures and worries in the smooth, rocking motions of your own private hammock.

This hammock stand is large enough to accommodate even an extra–wide hammock, like the one above. Its wide, sturdy base and firm uprights make it virtually impossible to overturn, even when you're rocking away at full tilt.

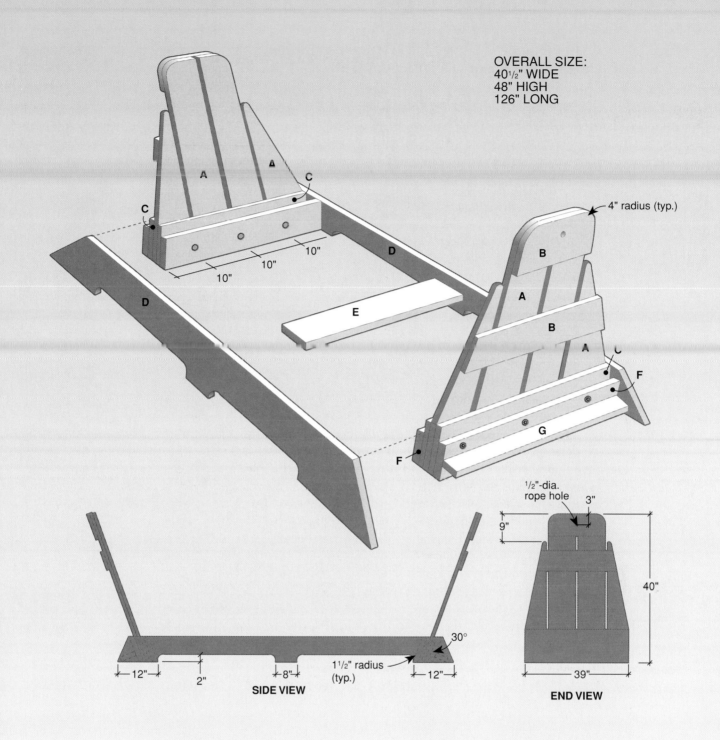

OVERALL SIZE:
40½" WIDE
48" HIGH
126" LONG

4" radius (typ.)

10"
10"
10"
10"

½"-dia.
rope hole

3"

9"

40"

39"

SIDE VIEW

12"
2"
8"
12"

1½" radius
(typ.)

30°

END VIEW

Cutting List				
Key	Part	Dimension	Pcs.	Material
A	End panel slat	¾ × 9¼ × 48"	8	Pine
B	Upper cross tie	¾ × 7¼ × 39"	4	Pine
C	Lower cross tie	¾ × 9¼ × 39"	4	Pine
D	Side rail	¾ × 7¼ × 105"	2	Pine

Cutting List				
Key	Part	Dimension	Pcs.	Material
E	Stringer	¾ × 7¼ × 39"	1	Pine
F	Standard brace	1½ × 7¼ × 39"	4	Pine
G	Rear brace	1½ × 3½ × 39"	2	Pine

Materials: Deck screws (1¼", 2", 2½"), ⅜ × 6" carriage bolts with washers and nuts, finishing materials.

Note: Measurements reflect the actual size of dimensional lumber.

81

Directions:
Hammock Stand

ASSEMBLE THE STANDARDS. The standards are the slat assemblies at the ends of the stand that support the hammock. Our strategy for building them is to join the 1 × 10 slats together, then cut them to shape as if they were one workpiece. First, cut the end panel slats (A) and lower panel cross ties (C) to length from 1 × 10 pine. Cut the upper panel cross ties (B) to length from 1 × 8 pine. Using the cutoff scraps as spacers, lay out the slats on a flat surface to form a 48 × 39" panel with ¾" spacing between the slats. Depending on the actual width of the 1 × 10 material (9¼" is typical), you may have to adjust the spacing between the slats to make the panel 39" wide. Lay one lower panel cross tie across the bottom of the panel, flush with the bottoms of the slats—use a square to make sure the slats are perpendicular to the cross tie. Fasten the lower cross tie to each slat with two 1¼" deck screws. Measure up from the bottom edge of the lower cross tie 20", and mark a line across the slats. Position one upper panel cross tie on the layout line, and the other flush with the top ends of the slats. Fasten the slats to the cross ties with deck screws. Attach slats to cross ties to make 39 × 48" panels for both standards.

TIP

If you already own a hammock that you wish to use, take measurements before building a stand. Adjust the dimensions of the stand, if necessary, to fit your hammock. The hammock stand shown here will hold even large hammocks with crosspieces up to 4' wide and 7' apart. The distance between the tops of the standards should be at least 3' longer than the space between hammock crosspieces.

Cut the end panel taper using a straight-line cutting jig and circular saw. Be sure to stop the cut at the inside slats.

Drive additional 2" screws from the front and back to draw the lower cross-ties tightly against the slats that make up the standards.

CUT & SHAPE THE STANDARDS. On the side of one panel that has no cross ties attached, measure down 9" on the inside edge of each outer slat and place a mark. Draw straight lines connecting each mark with the point where the top of the lower cross tie meets the outside edge of each outer slat. Cut along this line with a circular saw and straightedge **(photo A),** cutting through the cross ties as well as the end panel slats. Make similar cuts on both edges of both stan-

dards. Also cut roundovers at the top corners of the standards (see page 83) with a jig saw, then sand smooth with a belt sander and medium-grit (#100 to 120) sandpaper. Smooth out the pointed tips of the outer slats, then turn the standards over and attach lower cross ties, flush with the bottom edges of the standards. For extra strength, drive a few 2" deck screws through each cross-tie to draw the cross ties together **(photo B).**

MAKE THE SIDE RAILS & BRACE COMPONENTS. Cut the side rails (D) to length from 1 × 8 lumber. Measure in from each top end 5¼", and draw cutting lines that connect with the corner at the opposite edge. Cut along the lines with a circular saw **(photo C).** To create feet in the side rails, lay out and cut a pair of 2"-deep cutouts in the bottoms of the rails (see page 83). Cut the stringer (E) to size from 1 × 8 lumber; cut the standard braces (F) from 2 × 8 lumber; and cut the rear braces (G) from 2 × 4 lumber.

ASSEMBLE THE HAMMOCK STAND. At the ends of the side rails, draw 30° reference lines pointing in the opposite direction from the 30° bevels at the ends of the rails. Use the reference lines as guides for attaching the standard braces at a 30° angle between the side rails at each end of the hammock stand (see page 83). Use 2" deck screws and glue to attach the standard braces. Attach the rear braces behind the standard braces for extra support. Then, set a pair of 2¼" spacers against the inside face of each standard brace, and use them to set the gap for installing the inner standard braces **(photo D).** The standards are inserted between the standard braces. Install inner standard braces at both ends of the side rails. Position the stringer at the midpoint of the side rails, 3" down from the top edges, and attach with 2" deck screws. Set the standards into the standard brace slots at each end of the assembly. Drill three evenly spaced ⅜"-dia. holes through each standard/standard brace assembly, about 1" down from the tops of the braces. Insert

6"-long carriage bolts and secure with washers and nuts to hold the standards in place.

APPLY THE FINISHING TOUCHES. Measure down 3" from the top of each standard, and mark a drilling point on each upper cross tie, between the two middle slats. Drill a ½"-dia. hole for the hammock rope at each point.

Sand all edges and surfaces, and apply finish. We used light wood stain and water-based polyurethane (exterior-rated). Hang your hammock in the stand by threading the cords through the holes in the standards and tying a doubled square knot at the end of the rope. Pull the rope as taut as you can before tying the knot—hammocks will sag when put to use.

TIP

Water-based polyurethane is a durable topcoating product that is relatively easy to use. For best results, apply polyurethane in several light coats, buffing with a fine abrasive pad between coats.

Mark points 5¼" in from each side-rail end, then draw cutting lines between the points and the corner on the opposite edge of the rail.

Attach outer cross ties at a 30° angle, then attach the back cleats. Insert 2¼" spacers to set the gap between outer and inner cross ties.

Grill Garage

*Eliminate mess and clutter and shelter grilling appliances
from the elements with this spacious grill garage.*

CONSTRUCTION MATERIALS	
Quantity	**Lumber**
2	⅜" × 4 × 8' textured cedar sheet siding
1	¾" × 2 × 2' plywood
10	1 × 2" × 8' cedar

Summer cookouts will be more enjoyable with this handy grill garage and storage unit. Unlike most prefabricated grill garages, this project is sized to house today's popular gas grills, as well as traditional charcoal grills, when they are not being used. And while you are using your grill, the spacious top platforms of the grill garage can be used as staging and serving areas for your convenience. The walls of this grill garage are made from inexpensive, attractive rough cedar siding panels. Fitted with a cabinet-style door, the storage compartment can accommodate two large bags of charcoal, plus all your grilling accessories.

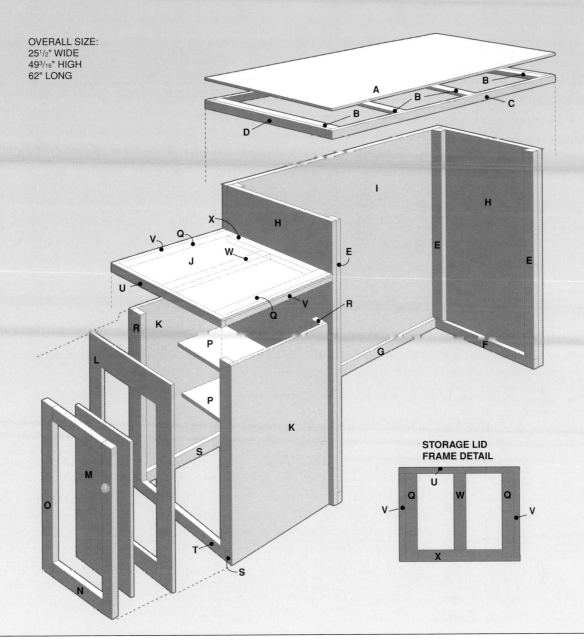

OVERALL SIZE:
25½" WIDE
49³⁄₁₆" HIGH
62" LONG

STORAGE LID FRAME DETAIL

Key	Part	Dimension	Pcs.	Material
A	Garage lid	⁷⁄₁₆ × 25½ × 43⅝"	1	Cedar siding
B	Lid stringer	¾ × 1½ × 24"	4	Cedar
C	Lid-frame side	¾ × 1½ × 43⅝"	2	Cedar
D	Lid-frame end	¾ × 1½ × 24"	2	Cedar
E	Posts	¾ × 1½ × 46½"	4	Cedar
F	End plate	¾ × 1½ × 23⁹⁄₁₆"	2	Cedar
G	Back plate	¾ × 1½ × 39¾"	1	Cedar
H	End panel	⁷⁄₁₆ × 24 × 48"	2	Cedar siding
I	Back panel	⁷⁄₁₆ × 41¼ × 48"	1	Cedar siding
J	Storage lid	⁷⁄₁₆ × 20 × 24"	1	Cedar siding
K	Side panel	⁷⁄₁₆ × 18 × 29¼"	2	Cedar siding
L	Face panel	⁷⁄₁₆ × 22½ × 29¼"	1	Cedar siding

Key	Part	Dimension	Pcs.	Material
M	Door panel	⁷⁄₁₆ × 18½ × 23¼"	1	Cedar siding
N	Door rail	¾ × 1½ × 17"	2	Cedar
O	Door stile	¾ × 1½ × 24¾"	2	Cedar
P	Shelf	¾ × 10 × 21⅝"	2	Plywood
Q	End stringer	¾ × 1½ × 19¼"	2	Cedar
R	Short post	¾ × 1½ × 27¾"	4	Cedar
S	Side plate	¾ × 1½ × 17⅛"	2	Cedar
T	Front plate	¾ × 1½ × 20⅛"	1	Cedar
U	Front lid edge	¾ × 1½ × 24"	1	Cedar
V	Storage lid end	¾ × 1½ × 19¼"	2	Cedar
W	Center stringer	¾ × 1½ × 17¾"	1	Cedar
X	Rear lid edge	¾ × 1½ × 19½"	1	Cedar

Cutting List

Materials: Moisture-resistant glue, deck screws (1", 1½", 2", 3"), hinges, door pull, finishing materials.

Note: Measurements reflect actual thickness of dimensional lumber.

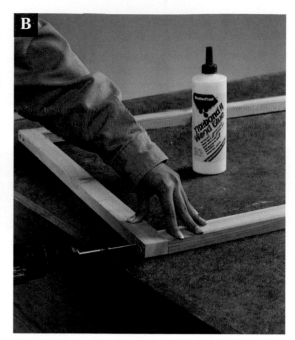

Install stringers inside the garage-lid frame to strengthen the garage lid.

Use 1 × 2 posts to create the framework for the main garage compartment.

Directions: Grill Garage

MAKE THE GARAGE LID PANEL. Cut the garage lid (A), to size from a cedar siding panel. Cut the lid stringers (B), lid-frame sides (C) and lid-frame ends (D), to size from 1 × 2 cedar. On a flat worksurface, arrange the frame ends and sides on edge to form the lid frame. Fasten the lid edges and lid ends together with glue and 1½" deck screws driven through the sides and into the ends of the lid-frame ends. Position the lid stringers facedown inside the frame, with one on each end and two spaced evenly between them. Fasten the stringers to the frame with glue and screws **(photo A).** Turn the frame over so the side where the stringers are flush with the top edges of the

frame is facing up. Lay the garage lid on top of the frame assembly and test the fit—the edges of the lid should be flush with the edges of the frame. Remove the garage lid and run a bead of glue on the top edges of the frame. Reposition the lid on the frame assembly and fasten with 1" deck screws driven through counterbored pilot holes in the lid and into the tops of the frame members.

BUILD THE GARAGE WALLS. Cut the posts (E) and end plates (F) to length from 1 × 2 cedar. Cut the end panels (H) to size from textured cedar sheet siding. Use a straightedge cutting guide whenever cutting sheet goods. Assemble an end plate and two posts into an open-end frame on your worksurface, and fasten the parts together with glue and screws driven through the posts and into the ends of the end plate **(photo B).** Test the fit, then attach an end panel to the

frame with glue and counterbored screws **(photo C).** Build the other end panel the same way.

ASSEMBLE THE GARAGE PANELS. Connect the end-panel assemblies with the back panel to create the walls for the main garage compartment. Cut the back plate (G) to length from 1 × 2 cedar, and cut the back panel (I) to size from textured cedar sheet siding. Stand one end-panel assembly up so it rests on the plate, and place a bead of glue along the edge of the post that will join the back panel. Position one end of the back panel flush against the post, making sure the rough side of the cedar siding is facing out. Attach the back panel to the end-panel assembly with 1½" screws. Attach the other end-panel assembly to the other side of the back panel the same way **(photo D).** Place

Attach the end panel to the open-ended frame assembly, making sure that the rough side of the cedar siding is facing outward.

a bead of glue along the outside face of the back plate and position the plate at the bottom of the back panel, so the ends of the plate form butt joints with the end-panel assemblies. Secure with 1" screws driven through the back panel and into the back plate. Fit the garage lid panel around the tops of the end and back panels, shifting the panels slightly as needed to create a tight fit. Attach the lid panel with glue and counterbored 2" deck screws driven through the lid frame and into the tops of the end and back panels.

BUILD THE CABINET LID. The cabinet is constructed with an open side that fits against the left end wall of the grill garage. Start by cutting the storage lid (J) to size from textured cedar sheet siding. Cut the end stringers (Q), center stringer (W), front lid edge (U), rear lid edge (X), and storage lid ends (V) to size from 1 × 2 cedar.

Lay the two storage lid ends and the front lid edge on edge on a flat surface. Position the storage lid ends so that they butt into the back face of the front lid edge. Fasten the ends and edge together with glue and 1½" screws. Lay the rear lid edge on its face between the end stringers, which are facedown, flush with the ends of the stringers. Mounting the rear lid edge in this manner will provide a flush fit at the rear of the storage unit assembly while maintaining an overhang on the sides and front. Fasten the rear lid edge and end stringers together with glue and 3" screws. Fasten the

storage-lid end/edge assembly to the end stringer/ rear-lid edge assembly with glue and screws to form a frame. Position the center stringer midway between the end stringers and attach with glue and screws. Turn the storage lid frame over so the side where the stringers are flush with the tops of the frame is facing up. Lay the storage lid panel on top of the frame to make sure the edges are flush, then attach the lid panel with glue and counterbored screws.

BUILD THE CABINET WALLS. Cut the short posts (R) and side plates (S) to length from 1 × 2 cedar. Then cut the side panels (K) to size from textured cedar sheet siding. Attach a side plate to the bottom, inside edge of a side panel, making sure the plate is flush with the front edge of the panel **(photo E)**. Attach a short post upright

Attach the back panel to the posts of the end panels to assemble the walls of the main grill garage compartment.

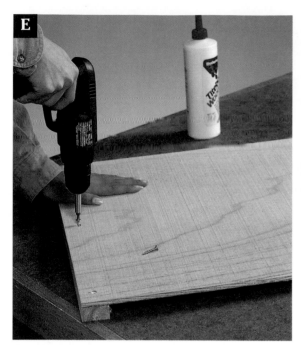

Attach the side plate, with the face against the panel, to the bottom edge of the side panel.

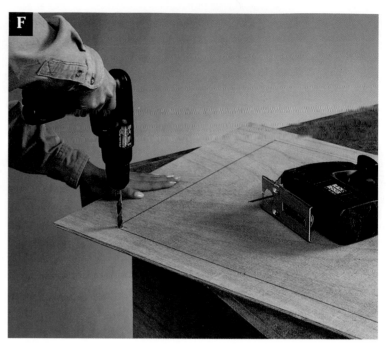

Drill a ³/₈"-dia. hole on the inside of one of the corners of the door layout, then cut out the door opening with a jig saw.

on the end of the side plate that is flush with the side panel, by driving a deck screw up through the plate and into the end of the post. Also drive a screw through the side panel and into the post. This post functions as a cleat for attaching the cabinet to the wall of the garage. Attach another short post in a similar position at the other side of the side panel. Build the second cabinet side panel the same way.

MAKE THE CABINET DOOR FACE FRAME. Cut the face-frame panel (L) from cedar siding. On the inside of the panel, mark a cutout for the cabinet door opening. First, measure down from the top 4", and draw a line across the panel. Then, measure in from both sides 2" and draw straight lines across the panel. Finally, draw a line 2" up from the bottom. The layout lines should form an 18½" × 23¼" rectangle. Drill a

⅜"-dia. starter hole for a jig saw blade at one corner of the cutout area **(photo F).** Cut out the door opening with a jig saw, then sand the edges smooth. Save the cutout piece: it can be used to make the door panel (M).

ASSEMBLE THE CABINET. Arrange the cabinet walls so they are 24½" apart, then attach the face frame to a short post on each wall, using glue and screws. Make sure the face frame is flush with the outside faces of the cabinet walls, and that the wide "rail" of the face frame is at the top of the cabinet, where there are no plates **(photo G).** Cut the front plate (T) and fasten it to the bottom, inside edge of the face frame, butted against the short posts. Place the cabinet lid assembly onto the cabinet walls and face frame, and attach the cabinet lid with glue and screws driven through the insides of the cabinet walls and into the frame of the lid **(photo H).**

MAKE & INSTALL THE SHELVES. Start by cutting the shelves (P) to size from plywood. Lay out ¾ × 1½" notches in the back corners of the shelves so they fit around the cabinet posts that cleat the top to the garage wall. Cut out the notches in the shelves, using a jig saw. On the inside of each cabinet wall, draw lines 8" down from the top and 11" up from the bottom to mark shelf locations. Fit the shelf notches around the back posts, then attach the shelves by driving deck screws through the cabinet sides and into the edges of the shelves—drive at least two screws into each shelf edge.

ATTACH THE CABINET TO THE GARAGE. Push the cabinet flush against the left wall of the garage. Fasten the cabinet to the garage with deck screws driven through the garage posts and into the short posts of the cabinet. Three screws into each post will provide sufficient holding power.

Fasten the cutout face frame to the cabinet sides.

Set the cabinet-lid assembly over the cabinet walls and face frame, then fasten with glue and screws

Fasten the door rails and door stiles to the door panel using glue and screws, leaving a ¾" overlap on all sides of the door panel.

APPLY THE FINISHING TOUCHES. Sand and smooth out the edges of the grill garage and prepare it for the finish of your choice. Since it is constructed with cedar, we chose a clear wood sealer that does not alter the rich wood grain and color. If you prefer a painted finish, be sure to use a quality primer and durable exterior enamel paint.

BUILD & ATTACH THE DOORS. Cut the door rails (N) and stiles (O) to length from 1 × 2 cedar. Using the cutout from the face frame panel (page 88) for the door panel (M), fasten the rails and stiles to the door panel using glue and screws. Leave a ¾" overlap on all sides

(photo I). Be sure to mount the rails between the stiles, but flush with the stile ends. Attach door hinges 3" from the top and bottom of the one door stile, then mount the door to the face frame. Install the door pull.

> **TIP**
>
> The grill garage is designed as a handy storage center for your grill and supplies, such as charcoal and cooking utensils. Do not store heavy items on top of the garage lid, and never light your grill while it is still in the grill garage. Do not store lighter fluid in the grill garage— always keep lighter fluid out of reach of children in a cool, sheltered area, like a basement.

PROJECT
POWER TOOLS

Picnic Table For Two

Turn a quiet corner of your yard into an intimate setting for dining alfresco with this compact picnic table.

CONSTRUCTION MATERIALS

Quantity	Lumber
1	2 × 8" × 6' cedar
1	2 × 6" × 8' cedar
3	2 × 4" × 8' cedar
3	1 × 6" × 8' cedar
3	1 × 2" × 8' cedar

A picnic table doesn't have to be a clumsy, uncomfortable family feeding trough. In this project, we created a unique picnic table that's just the right size for two people to enjoy. Portable and lightweight, it can be set in a corner of your garden, beneath a shade tree or on your deck or patio to enhance your outdoor dining experiences. The generously proportioned tabletop can be set with full table settings for a formal meal in the garden, but it is intimate enough for sharing a cool beverage with a special person as you watch the sun set. Made with plain dimensional cedar, this picnic table for two is sturdy and long-lasting as well.

OVERALL SIZE:
28" HIGH
30" WIDE
68" LONG

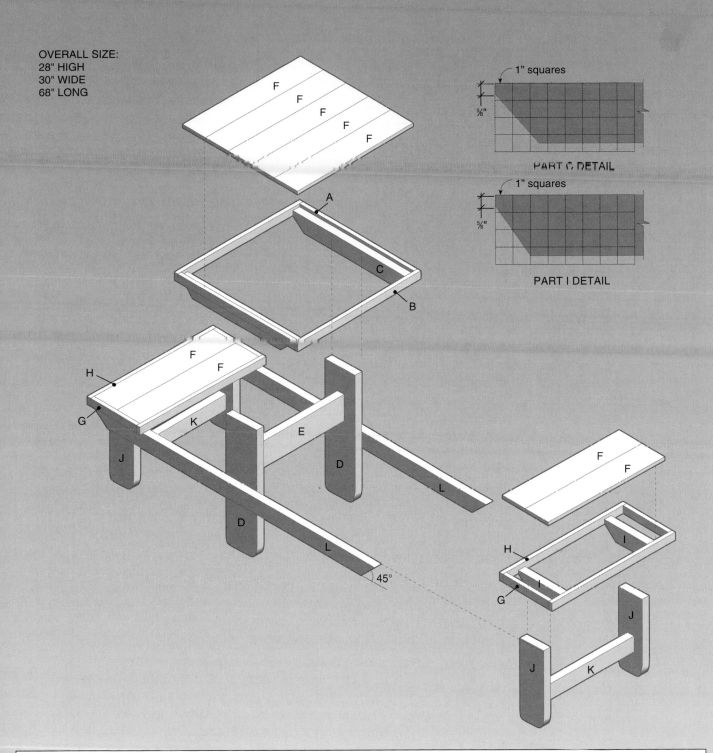

PART C DETAIL

PART I DETAIL

1" squares

1" squares

5/8"

5/8"

45°

Cutting List				
Key	Part	Dimension	Pcs.	Material
A	Tabletop frame	7/8 × 1½ × 27¾"	2	Cedar
B	Tabletop frame	7/8 × 1½ × 30"	2	Cedar
C	Table stringer	1½ × 3½ × 27¾"	2	Cedar
D	Table leg	1½ × 7¼ × 27¼"	2	Cedar
E	Table stretcher	1½ × 5½ × 22¼"	1	Cedar
F	Slat	7/8 × 5½ × 28¼"	9	Cedar

Cutting List				
Key	Part	Dimension	Pcs.	Material
G	Bench frame	7/8 × 1½ × 11¼"	4	Cedar
H	Bench frame	7/8 × 1½ × 30"	4	Cedar
I	Bench stringer	1½ × 3½ × 11¼"	4	Cedar
J	Bench leg	1½ × 5½ × 15¼"	4	Cedar
K	Bench stretcher	1½ × 3½ × 22¼"	2	Cedar
L	Cross rail	1½ × 3½ × 68"	2	Cedar

Materials: Moisture-resistant glue, brass or galvanized deck screws (1⅝", 2½"), finishing materials.

Note: Measurements reflect the actual size of dimensional lumber.

Make triangular cutoffs at the ends on the table stringers, using a circular saw.

Install the tabletop slats by driving screws through the tabletop frame and into the ends of the slats.

Directions:
Picnic Table For Two

BUILD THE TABLETOP. The tabletop for the picnic table is made from 1 × 6 cedar slats wrapped with a 1 × 2 frame. Start by cutting the tabletop frame pieces (A, B), the table stringers (C) and the table slats (F). Sand the parts, then mark triangular cutoffs at each end of the stringers by drawing cutting lines that start 2½" in from one end and connect with a point at the same end, ⅝" in from the opposite edge of the board (see *Diagram*, page 9). Miter-cut along the lines with a circular saw to make the cutoffs **(photo A).** Fasten the shorter tabletop frame pieces (A) to the sides of the stringers. The tops of the frame pieces should extend ⅞" above the tops of the stringers, and the ends should be flush. Use moisture-resistant glue and 1⅝" deck screws to attach the frame pieces to the stringers. Drive the screws through countersunk pilot holes. Then, position the longer tabletop frame pieces (B) so they overlay the

ends of the shorter frame pieces, and fasten them together with glue and screws to complete the frames. Next, set the slats inside the frame so the ends of the slats rest on the stringers. Space them evenly, about ⅜" apart. Drive two screws through countersunk pilot holes in the tabletop frame, and into the end of each slat, starting with the two end slats **(photo B).**

MAKE & ATTACH THE TABLE-LEG ASSEMBLY. Two legs with rounded bottoms are attached to the centers of the stringers to support the tabletop. A single stretcher is attached between the legs for stability. Cut the table legs (D) and table stretcher (E). Use a compass to draw a roundover curve with a 1½" radius on the corners of one end of each leg. These ends will be the bottoms of the legs. Cut the curves with a jig saw. Press an end of the stretcher against the inside face of one of the table legs, 16" up from the bottom of the leg and centered side to side. Trace the outline of the stretcher onto the leg, and repeat the procedure

on the other leg. Drill two evenly spaced pilot holes through the stretcher outlines on the legs, and countersink the holes on the outside faces of the legs. Attach the stretcher with glue and 2½" deck screws driven through the pilot holes and into the ends of the stretcher. To attach the table-leg assembly, turn the tabletop upside down, and apply glue to the table stringers where they will contact the legs. Position the legs in place within the tabletop frame, and attach them by driving 2½" deck screws through the legs and into the table stringers **(photo C).**

BUILD THE BENCH TOPS. The bench tops are very similar in design to the tabletop. Start by cutting the bench frame pieces (G, H) and bench stringers (I). Miter-cut the ends of the bench stringers in the same way you cut the table stringers, starting ⅝" down from the top edge and 2" in from the ends on the bottom edges. Assemble the frame pieces into two rectangular frames by driving screws through the longer frame

Position the table legs inside the tabletop frame, and attach them to the table stringers.

Set the bench legs against the outer faces of the stringers. Attach the legs to the stringers, then attach the stretcher between the legs.

pieces and into the ends of the shorter frame pieces. Turn the bench frames upside down, and center the bench slats inside them so the outer edges of the slats are flush against the frame. Attach the slats by driving 1⅝" deck screws through the frames and into the ends of the slats. Attach the stringers inside the frame so the tops of the stringers are flat against the undersides of the slats, 3" in from each frame end. Use glue and 1⅝" deck screws driven through the angled ends of the stringers and into the undersides of the slats. Be careful to locate the screws so they are far enough away from the ends of the stringers that they do not stick out through the tops of the slats after they are driven. The stringers are not attached directly to the bench frames.

BUILD THE BENCH LEGS. Start by cutting the bench legs (J) and bench stretchers (K). Use a compass to draw a roundover curve with a 1½" radius on the corners of one end of each leg. Cut the roundovers with a jig saw. Center the tops of the bench legs against the outside

faces of the bench stringers. Attach the bench legs to the bench stringers with glue and countersunk 2½" deck screws, driven through the stringers and into the legs. Position the bench stretchers against the inside faces of the bench legs, 3½" up from the bench leg bottoms. Glue the bench stretchers, and attach them between the legs with countersunk 2½" deck screws **(photo D).**

JOIN THE TABLE & BENCHES. Cut the cross rails (L) to length, miter-cutting the ends at a 45° angle (see *Diagram*). Position the benches so the ends of the cross rails are flush with the outside ends of the bench frames. Apply glue, and attach the cross rails to the bench legs with countersunk 2½" deck screws. Stand the benches up, and cen-

ter the table legs between the cross rails. Apply glue to the joints between cross rails and legs, then clamp the table legs to the cross rails, making sure the parts are perpendicular **(photo E).** Secure the parts by driving several 2½" deck screws through the cross rails and into the outside face of each leg.

APPLY FINISHING TOUCHES. Sand all the sharp edges and flat surfaces of the picnic table, then apply a nontoxic wood sealant to protect the wood and keep it from turning gray.

Center the table within the cross rails, and clamp it in place.

93

Park Bench

This attention-grabbing park bench is a real showpiece that can transform even a plain yard into a formal garden.

CONSTRUCTION MATERIALS

Quantity	Lumber
5	2 × 4" × 8' pine
1	2 × 2" × 4' pine
4	1 × 6" × 8' pine

Add color and style to your backyard or garden with this bright, elegant park bench. Some careful jig saw work is all it takes to make the numerous curves and contours that give this bench a sophisticated look. But don't worry if your cuts aren't all perfect: the shapes are decorative, so the bench will still work just fine. In fact, if you prefer a simpler appearance, you can build the park bench with all straight parts, except the roundovers at the bottoms of the legs. But if you are willing to do the extra work, you're sure to be pleased with the final result—we certainly were, and that's why we finished it with bright red paint so no one would miss it.

OVERALL SIZE:
38" HIGH
23" DEEP
52" LONG

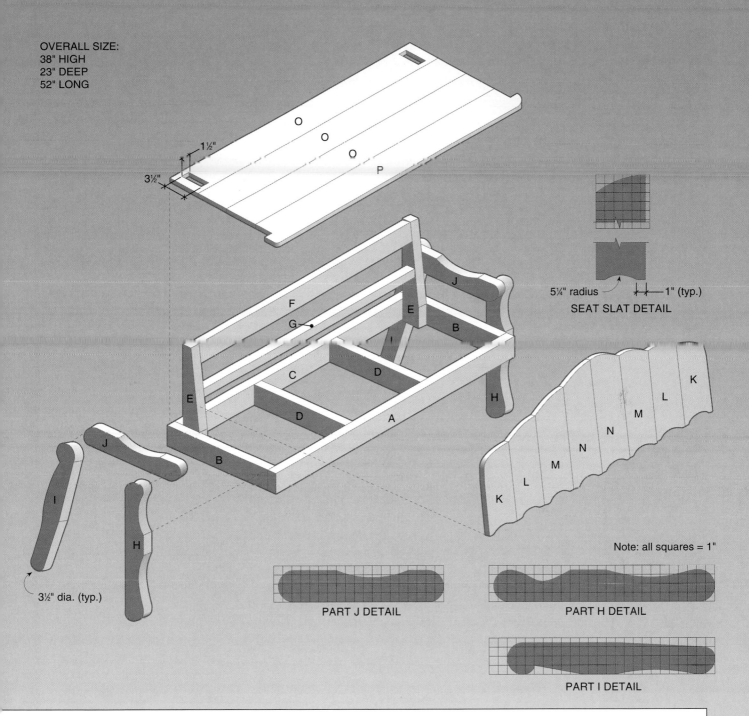

1½"

3½"

5¼" radius — 1" (typ.)

SEAT SLAT DETAIL

Note: all squares = 1"

3½" dia. (typ.)

PART J DETAIL

PART H DETAIL

PART I DETAIL

Cutting List				
Key	Part	Dimension	Pcs.	Material
A	Front rail	1½ × 3½ × 49"	1	Pine
B	Side rail	1½ × 3½ × 20¼"	2	Pine
C	Back rail	1½ × 3½ × 46"	1	Pine
D	Cross rail	1½ × 3½ × 18¾"	2	Pine
E	Post	1½ × 3½ × 18"	2	Pine
F	Top rail	1½ × 3½ × 43"	1	Pine
G	Bottom rail	1½ × 1½ × 43"	1	Pine
H	Front leg	1½ × 3½ × 24½"	2	Pine

Cutting List				
Key	Part	Dimension	Pcs.	Material
I	Rear leg	1½ × 3½ × 23"	2	Pine
J	Armrest	1½ × 3½ × 18½"	2	Pine
K	End slat	¾ × 5½ × 14"	2	Pine
L	Outside slat	¾ × 5½ × 16"	2	Pine
M	Inside slat	¾ × 5½ × 18"	2	Pine
N	Center slat	¾ × 5½ × 20"	2	Pine
O	Seat slat	¾ × 5½ × 49"	3	Pine
P	Seat nose slat	¾ × 5½ × 52"	1	Pine

Materials: Moisture-resistant glue, deck screws (1¼", 2½"), finishing materials.

Note: All measurements reflect the actual size of dimensional lumber.

Use a router or sander to round over the sharp bottom edges and corners of the completed seat frame.

Attach the seat slats and nose slat to the top of the seat frame with glue and deck screws.

Directions: Park Bench

BUILD THE SEAT FRAME. The seat frame is made by assembling rails and cross rails to form a rectangular unit. Start by cutting the front rail (A), side rails (B), back rail (C) and cross rails (D) to size. Sand all the parts with medium-grit sandpaper to smooth out any rough spots after cutting. Fasten the side rails to the front rail with moisture-resistant glue and 2½" deck screws, driven through the front rail and into the side rail ends. Counterbore the pilot holes to accept ⅜"-dia. wood plugs. Make sure the top and bottom edges of the side rails are flush with the top and bottom edges of the front rails. Attach the back rail between the side rails with glue and counterbored deck screws, driven through the side rails and into the ends of the back rail. Keep the back

rail flush with the ends of the side rails. Use glue and deck screws to fasten the two cross rails between the front and back rails, 14½" in from the inside face of each side rail. These cross rails provide structural support and help support the seat slats, which are attached to the top of the frame later in the assembly process. Complete the seat frame by rounding the bottom edges and corners with a router and a ⅜"-dia. roundover bit **(photo A)** or a hand sander.

MAKE THE SEAT SLATS. The very front seat slat, called the nose slat, has side cutouts to accept the front legs, and the back seat slat has cutouts, called mortises, to accept the posts that support the backrest.

Start by cutting the seat nose slat (P) and one seat slat (O) to size. To mark the 2 × 4 cutout at each end of the nose slat, use the end of a 2 × 4 as a template. Position the 2 × 4 on the seat slat at each end, 1½" in from the back edge and 1½" in from the end. The long sides of the 2 × 4 should be parallel to the ends of the back seat slat. Trace the outline of the 2 × 4 onto the slat. Drill a starter hole within the outline, and make the cutout with a jig saw. Then, use a jig saw to cut a 3"-long × 1½"-wide notch at each end of the nose slat, starting at the back edge (see *Diagram*, page 13). Sand the notches and mortises with a file or a thin sanding block. Use a router with roundover bit to shape the front edge of the nose slat.

ATTACH THE SEAT SLATS. The seat slats are attached to the top of the seat frame, parallel to the front and back rails. Cut the rest of the seat slats (O) to size,

TIP

Making smooth contour cuts with a jig saw can be a little tricky. To make it easier, install fairly thick saw blades, because they are less likely to "wander" with the grain of the wood. Using a scrolling jig saw will also help, since they are easier to turn than standard jig saws.

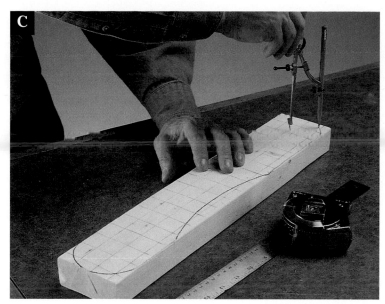

After drawing a 1" grid on the legs and armrests, draw the finished shape of the parts, following the Grid Patterns on page 95.

then lay the slats on the seat frame so the ends of the slats are flush with the frame, and the nose slat overhangs equally at the sides of the frame. Draw reference lines onto the tops of the seat slats and nose slat, directly over the top of each rail in the frame. These lines will be used to mark drilling points before attaching the slats to the seat frame. Mark two drilling points on each line on each slat, ¾" in from the front and from the back of the slat. Drill counterbored pilot holes at the drilling points. Sand the seat slats and nose slat, and attach them to the seat frame with glue and 1¼" deck screws **(photo B),** driven through the slats and into the frame and cross rails. Start with the front and back slats, and space the inner slats evenly.

MAKE THE LEGS & ARMRESTS. The front legs (H), rear legs (I) and armrests (J) are shaped using the Grid Patterns on page 13. First, cut workpieces for the parts to the full sizes shown in

the *Cutting List*. Use a pencil to draw a 1"-square grid pattern on each workpiece. Then, use the grid patterns as a reference for drawing the shapes onto the workpieces **(photo C)**—it will help if you enlarge the patterns on a photocopier or draw them to a larger scale on a piece of graph paper first. Cut out the shapes with a jig saw, then sand the contour cuts smooth. Use a drum sander mounted in your electric drill for best sanding results.

ATTACH THE LEGS. The front and rear legs are attached to the armrests, flush with the front and rear ends. Use glue and counterbored deck screws to fasten the front legs to the outside faces of the armrests, using a framing square

to make sure the legs are perpendicular to the armrests. Temporarily fasten the rear legs to the outside faces of the armrests with a centered, counterbored screw, driven through the rear leg and into the armrest. The rear leg must, for now, remain adjustable on the armrest. Once the rear legs have been positioned correctly against the seat, you will attach them permanently to the armrests. Clamp the seat to the legs. The front of the edge of the seat should be 16¾" up from the bottoms of the front legs. The back of the seat should be 14¼" up from the bottoms of the rear legs. Position square wood spacers between the seat and each armrest to keep the armrest parallel to the frame. Adjust the rear legs so their back edges are flush with the top corners of the side rails. The rear legs extend slightly beyond the back of the seat frame. Drive counterbored deck screws through the front and rear legs and into the side rails, then

Carefully clamp the leg frames to the seat, and attach them with glue and counterbored screws.

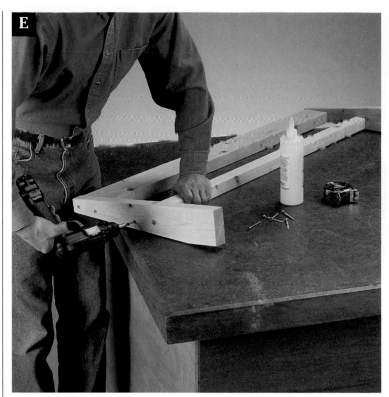

Glue the ends of the top and bottom rails, then drive deck screws through the posts to attach them to the rails.

The top front corner of the top rail should be flush with the top of the posts. Position the bottom rail between the posts so its bottom edge is 9" up from the bottoms of the posts. Make sure the front face of the bottom rail is flush with the front edges of the posts. Attach the parts with glue and counterbored 2½" deck screws **(photo E).** Use a router with a ⅜"-dia. roundover bit, or a hand sander, to round over the back edges of the back frame.

MAKE THE BACK SLATS. The back slats are shaped on their tops and bottoms to create a scalloped effect when they are attached. Keep in mind, if you'd rather not spend the time cutting these contours, you can simply cut the slats to length and round over the top edges. Start by cutting the end slats (K), outside slats (L), inside slats (M) and center slats (N) to length. Draw a 1"-square grid pattern on one slat, then draw the shape shown in the *Slat Detail* on page 13 onto the slat. Then, mark a 5¼"-radius scalloped cutout at the bottom of the slat, using a compass. Cut the slat to shape with a jig saw, and sand smooth any rough spots or saw marks. Use the completed slat as a template to trace the same profile on the tops and bottoms of the remaining slats **(photo F),** and cut them to shape with a jig saw. Sand the cuts smooth.

ATTACH THE BACK SLATS. Before attaching the back slats to the back frame, clamp a straight board across the fronts of the posts with its top edge 8½" up from the bottoms of the posts **(photo G).** Using this board as a guide will make it easy to keep the slats aligned

drive an additional screw through each rear leg into the armrests to permanently secure the rear legs in position. Unclamp the leg assemblies, and remove them from the frame **(photo D).** Apply glue to the leg assemblies where they join the frame, and reattach the legs and armrests using the same screw holes.

BUILD THE BACK FRAME. The back frame is made by attaching a top rail (F) and bottom rail (G) between two posts (E).

Once the back frame has been built, it is inserted into the mortises in the rear seat slats to form a backrest. Before you attach the rails, cut tapers on the front edges of the posts. The tapered posts will create a backward slope so the back slats make a more comfortable backrest when they are attached. When you attach the rails between the posts, make sure they are flush with the front edges of the posts. Cut the posts, top rail and bottom rail to size. Mark a tapered cutting line on each post, starting 1½" in from the back edge, at the top. Extend the line so it meets the front edge 3½" up from the bottom. Cut the taper in each post, using a circular saw or jig saw. Use glue and deck screws to fasten the top rail between the posts so the front face of the top rail is flush with the front (tapered) edge of each post.

Use the first completed back slat as a template for tracing cutting lines on the rest of the back slats.

Clamp a straight board to the back frame to help keep the back slats aligned along their bottom edges as you install them.

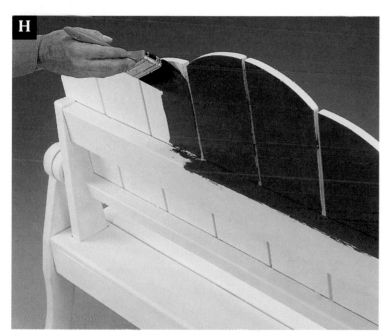

Apply two thin coats of exterior primer to seal the pine, then paint the park bench with two coats of enamel house trim paint.

as you attach them. Fasten the end slats to the back frame with glue and deck screws, making sure the bottoms are resting flat against the clamped guide board. (For more information on back slat positioning, see the *Diagram*, page 13.) Make sure the outside edges of

the end slats are flush with the outside edges of the posts. Attach the remaining slats between the end slats, spaced so the gaps are even.

ASSEMBLE THE BENCH. Attach the rear frame by sliding the back into place inside the notches in the rear seat slat.

The posts should rest against the back rail and side rails. Keep the bottoms of the posts flush with the bottom edges of the side rails. Drive counterbored, 2½" screws through the posts and into the side rails, and through the back rail and into the posts to secure the rear frame to the bench seat.

APPLY FINISHING TOUCHES. Apply moisture-resistant glue to ⅜"-dia. wood plugs, and insert them into each counterbored screw hole. Sand the plugs until they are flush with the wood. Sand all surfaces smooth with medium (100 or 120 grit) sandpaper, then finish-sand the project with fine (150 or 180 grit) sandpaper. Finish as desired; we used two thin coats of primer and two coats of exterior house trim paint **(photo H).** Whenever you use untreated pine for an outdoor project, it is very important that you apply an exterior-rated finish to protect the wood. Untreated pine is susceptible to rot and other forms of moisture damage.

Firewood Shelter

Those stacks of firewood won't be an eyesore anymore once you build this ranch-style firewood shelter for your yard.

Quantity	Lumber
8	2 × 4" × 8' cedar
5	2 × 6" × 8' cedar
10	⅜ × 8" × 8' cedar lap siding

This handsome firewood shelter combines rustic ranch styling with ample sheltered storage that keeps firewood off the ground and obscured from sight. Clad on the sides and roof with beveled cedar lap siding, the shelter has the look and feel of a permanent structure. But because it is freestanding, it can be moved around as needed, and requires no time-consuming foundation work.

This firewood shelter is large enough to hold an entire face cord of firewood. And since the storage area is sheltered and raised to avoid ground contact and allow air flow, wood dries quickly and is ready to use when you need it.

OVERALL SIZE:
62" HIGH
24" DEEP
8' LONG

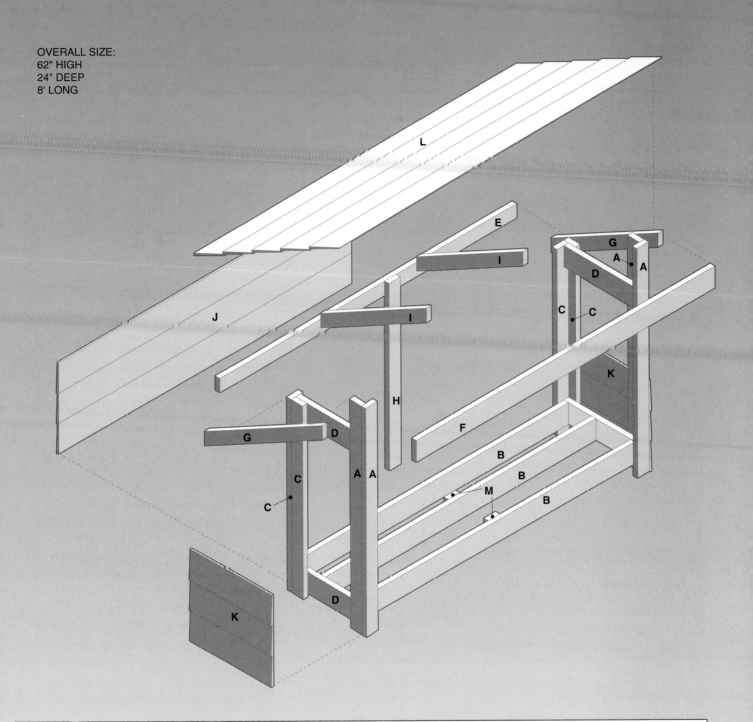

Cutting List				
Key	Part	Dimension	Pcs.	Material
A	Front post	1½ × 3½ × 59"	4	Cedar
B	Bottom rail	1½ × 5½ × 82½"	3	Cedar
C	Rear post	1½ × 3½ × 50"	4	Cedar
D	End rail	1½ × 5½ × 21"	4	Cedar
E	Back rail	1½ × 3½ × 88¾"	1	Cedar
F	Front rail	1½ × 5½ × 88¾"	1	Cedar
G	Roof support	1½ × 3½ × 33¾"	2	Cedar

Cutting List				
Key	Part	Dimension	Pcs.	Material
H	Middle post	1½ × 3½ × 50"	1	Cedar
I	Middle support	1½ × 3½ × 26½"	2	Cedar
J	Back siding	⅝ × 8 × 88¾"	3	Cedar siding
K	End siding	⅝ × 8 × 24"	6	Cedar siding
L	Roof strips	⅝ × 8 × 96"	5	Cedar siding
M	Prop	1½ × 3½ × 7½"	2	Cedar

Materials: ⅜ × 3½" lag screws (24), ⅜ × 4" lag screws (8), 1½" spiral siding nails, deck screws (2½", 3"), finishing materials,

Note: Measurements reflect the actual size of dimensional lumber.

Directions:
Firewood Shelter

BUILD THE FRAME. The basic framework for the firewood shelter is made of four corner posts, connected by end rails at the sides and full-width bottom rails. Cut the front posts (A) and rear posts (C). Butt the edges of the front posts together in pairs to form the corner posts. Join the post pairs with 2½" deck screws, driven through countersunk pilot holes at 8" intervals. Join the rear posts in pairs. Cut the bottom rails (B) and end rails (D). Assemble two bottom rails and two end rails into a rectangular frame,

with the end rails covering the ends of the bottom rails. Set the third bottom rail between the end rails, centered between the other bottom rails. Mark the ends of the bottom rails on the outside faces of the end rails. Drill a pair of ⅜"-dia. pilot holes for lag screws through the end rails at each bottom rail position—do not drill into the bottom rails. Drill a ¾"-dia. counterbore for each pilot hole, deep enough so the heads of the lag screws will be recessed. Drill a smaller, ¼"-dia. pilot hole through each pilot hole in the end rails, into the ends of the bottom rails **(photo A).** Drive a ⅜ × 3½" lag screw fitted with a washer at each pilot hole, using a socket wrench. Next, draw reference lines across the inside faces of the corner posts, 2" up from the bottoms. With the corner posts upright and about 82" apart, set 2"-high spacers next to each corner post to support the frame. Position the bottom rail frame between the corner posts, and attach the frame to the corner posts by driving two 2½" deck screws through the corner posts and into the outer

faces of the bottom rails. Drive a pair of ⅜ × 4" lag screws, fitted with washers, through the sides of the corner posts and into the bottom rails the lag screws need to go through the post and end rail, and into the end of the bottom rail, without hitting the lag screws that are already driven through the end rails. Drill counterbored pilot holes and drive the lag screws. Complete the frame by installing end rails at the tops of the corner posts, using countersunk 2½" deck screws. Make sure the tops of the end rails are flush with the tops of the rear posts **(photo B).**

MAKE THE ROOF FRAME. The roof is made from beveled cedar lap siding that is attached to a roof frame supported by the corner posts. Cut the back rail (E), front rail (F), roof supports (G), middle post (H) and middle supports (I) to length. The roof supports and middle supports are mitered at the ends. To make cutting lines for the miter cuts, mark a point 1½" in from each end, along the edge of the board. Draw diagonal lines from each point to the opposing corner. Cut along

Use a smaller bit to extend the pilot holes for the lag screws into the ends of the bottom rails.

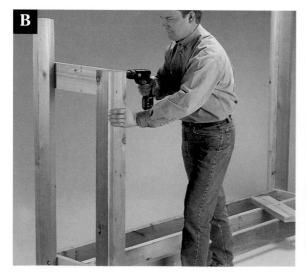

Attach end rails between front and rear corner posts.

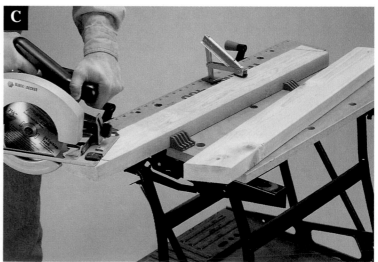

Miter-cut the middle supports and roof supports with a circular saw.

Attach the front rail by driving screws through the outer roof supports, making sure the top of the rail is flush with the tops of the supports.

Attach the middle roof supports by driving screws through the front and back rails.

the lines with a circular saw **(photo C).** Use countersunk 3" deck screws to fasten the back rail to the backs of the rear corner posts, flush with their tops and sides. Fasten a roof sup port to the outsides of the corner posts, using countersunk 3" deck screws, and making sure the top of each roof support is flush with the high point of each post end. The roof supports should overhang the posts equally in the front and rear. Use countersunk deck screws to attach the front rail between the roof supports **(photo D),** making sure the top is flush with the tops of the roof supports. Attach the middle supports between the front rail and back rail, 30" in from each rail end. Drive 3" deck screws through the front and back rails into the ends of the middle supports **(photo E).** Use a pipe clamp to hold the supports in place as you attach them. Next, position the middle post (H) so it fits against the outside of the rear bottom rail and the inside of the top back rail. Make sure the middle post is perpen-

dicular and extends past the bottom rail by 2", and attach it with countersunk 2½" deck screws. Finally, help keep the bottom rails from sagging under the weight of the firewood by cutting a pair of 2 × 4 props (M) to length and attaching them to the front two bottom rails, aligned with the middle post. Make sure the tops of the props are flush with the tops of the bottom rails.

ATTACH THE SIDING & ROOF. Cut pieces of 8"-wide beveled cedar lap siding to length to make the siding strips (J, K) and the roof strips (L). Starting 2" up from the bottoms of the rear posts, fasten the back siding strips (J) with two 1½" siding nails driven through each strip and into the posts, near the top and bottom edge of the strip. Work your way up, overlapping each piece of siding by ½", making sure the thicker edges of the beveled siding strips face down. Attach the end siding (K) to the corner posts, with the seams aligned with the seams in the back siding. Attach the roof strips (L) to

Attach the roof strips with siding nails, starting at the back edge and working your way forward.

the roof supports, starting at the back edge. Drive two nails into each roof support. Make sure the wide edge of the beveled siding faces down. Attach the rest of the roof strips, overlapping the strip below by about ½" **(photo F),** until you reach the front edges of the roof supports. You can leave the cedar wood untreated, or apply an exterior wood stain to keep the wood from turning gray as it weathers.

Trellis Planter

Two traditional yard furnishings are combined into one compact package.

The decorative trellis and the cedar planter are two staples found in many yards and gardens. By integrating the appealing shape and pattern of the trellis with the rustic, functional design of the cedar planter, this building project showcases the best qualities of both furnishings.

Because the 2 × 2 lattice trellis is attached to the planter, not permanently fastened to a wall or railing, the trellis planter can be moved easily to follow changing sunlight patterns, or to occupy featured areas of your yard. It is also easy to move for storage during non-growing seasons. You may even want to consider installing wheels or casters on the base for greater mobility.

Building the trellis planter is a very simple job. The trellis portion is made entirely of strips of 2 × 2 cedar, fashioned together in a crosshatch pattern. The planter bin is a basic wood box, with panel sides and a two-board bottom with drainage holes, that rests on a scalloped base. The trellis is screwed permanently to the back of the planter bin.

Stocking the trellis planter with plantings is a matter of personal taste and growing conditions. In most areas, ivy, clematis, and grapevines are good examples of climbing plants that can be trained up the trellis. Ask at your local gardening center for advice on plantings. Plants can be set into the bin in containers, or you can fill the bin with potting soil and plant directly in the bin.

CONSTRUCTION MATERIALS

Quantity	Lumber
1	2 × 6" × 8' cedar
1	2 × 4" × 6' cedar
4	2 × 2" × 8' cedar
2	1 × 6" × 8' cedar
1	1 × 2" × 6' cedar

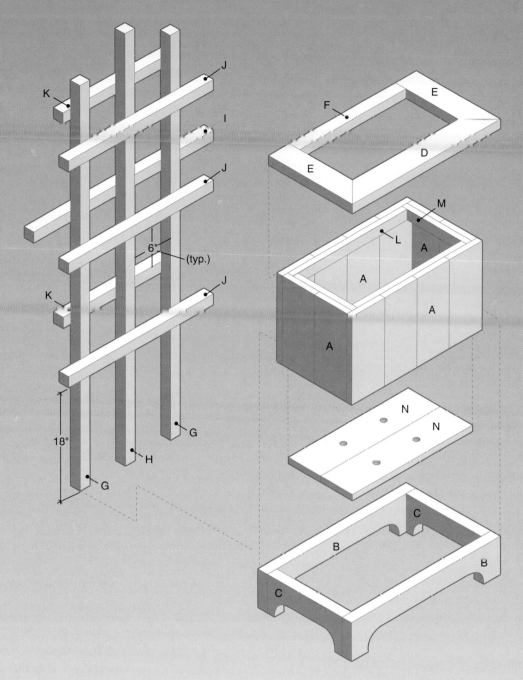

OVERALL SIZE:
69" HIGH
18¾" DEEP
30" LONG

6" (typ.)

18"

Cutting List

Key	Part	Dimension	Pcs.	Material
A	Box slat	⅞ × 5½ × 13"	12	Cedar
B	Base front/back	1½ × 5½ × 25"	2	Cedar
C	Base end	1½ × 5½ × 12¾"	2	Cedar
D	Cap front	1½ × 3½ × 25"	1	Cedar
E	Cap end	1½ × 3½ × 14¼"	2	Cedar
F	Cap back	1½ × 1½ × 18"	1	Cedar
G	End post	1½ × 1½ × 59½"	2	Cedar

Cutting List

Key	Part	Dimension	Pcs.	Material
H	Center post	1½ × 1½ × 63½"	1	Cedar
I	Long rail	1½ × 1½ × 30"	1	Cedar
J	Medium rail	1½ × 1½ × 24"	3	Cedar
K	Short rail	1½ × 1½ × 18"	2	Cedar
L	Cleat	⅞ × 1½ × 18¼"	2	Cedar
M	Cleat	⅞ × 1½ × 11"	2	Cedar
N	Bottom board	⅞ × 5½ × 20¼"	2	Cedar

Materials: Moisture-resistant wood glue, deck screws (1⅝", 2½"), finishing materials.

Note: Measurements reflect the actual size of dimensional lumber.

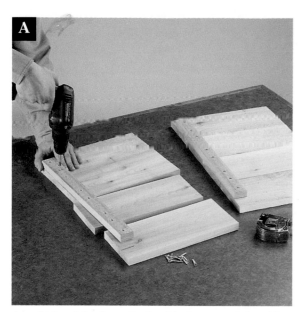

Attach the side cleats flush with the tops of the side boards.

Use a jig saw to make scalloped cutouts in all four base pieces—make sure the cutouts in matching pieces are the same.

Directions: Trellis Planter

BUILD THE PLANTER BIN. The planter bin is made by attaching side panels to end panels, forming a box. Each side panel is made of four 1 × 6 cedar slats, and each end panel is made of two 1 × 6 slats. Start by cutting the box slats (A) and cleats (L, M). Arrange the slats edge to edge in two groups of four and two groups of two, with the tops and bottoms flush in each group. Set a long cleat (L) at the top of each set of four slats, so the distance from each end of the cleat to the end of the panel is the same. Attach the cleats to the four-slat panels with 1⅝" deck screws **(photo A),** driven through the cleats and into the slats. Next, lay the short cleats (M) at the tops of the two-slat panels, and attach them to the slats the same way. Arrange all four panels into a box shape, apply moisture-resistant wood glue to the joints, and attach the panels with 1⅝" deck screws driven through the

four-slat panels and into the ends of the two-slat panels.

INSTALL THE BIN BOTTOM. Cut the bottom boards (N) to length. Set the bin upside down on your worksurface, and mark reference lines on the inside faces of the panels, ⅞" in from the bottom of the bin. Insert the bottom boards into the bin, aligned with the reference lines to create a ⅞" recess (scraps of 1× cedar can be slipped beneath the bottom boards as spacers). Fasten the bottom boards by driving 1⅝" deck screws through the panels, and into the edges and ends of the bottom boards. Countersink the screwheads slightly.

BUILD THE PLANTER BASE. The planter base is a frame that wraps around the bottom of the planter bin. The frame pieces are scalloped to create feet at the corners when the frame is assembled. Begin by cutting the base front and back (B) boards and the base ends (C). To draw the contours for the scallops on the front and

back boards, set the point of a compass at the bottom edge of the base front, 5" in from one end. Set the compass to a 2½" radius, and draw a curve to mark the curved end of the cutout (see *Diagram*). Draw a straight line to connect the tops of the curves, 2½" up from the bottom of the board, to complete the scalloped cutout. Make the cutout with a jig saw, then sand any rough spots in the cut. Use the board as a template for marking a matching cutout on the base back. Draw a similar cutout on one base end, except with the point of the compass 3½" in from the ends. Cut out both end pieces with a jig saw **(photo B).** Draw reference lines for countersunk wood screws, ¾" from the ends of the base sides. Drill three evenly spaced pilot holes through the lines. Fasten the base ends between the base front and back with three evenly spaced deck screws driven at each joint.

The recess beneath the bottom boards in the planter bin provides access for driving screws.

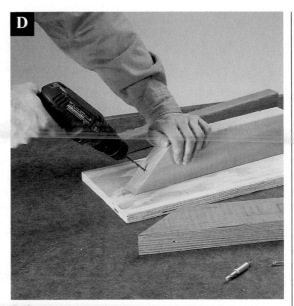

Before attaching the cap ends, drill pilot holes through the mitered ends of the cap front ends.

ATTACH THE BIN TO THE BASE. Set the base frame and planter bin on their back. Position the planter bin inside the base so it extends ⅞" past the top of the base. Drive 1⅝" deck screws through the planter bin and into the base to secure the parts **(photo C)**.

MAKE THE CAP FRAME. The top of the bin is wrapped with a wood cap. Cut the cap front (D), cap ends (E) and cap back (F) to length. Cut 45° miters at one end of each cap end, and at both ends of the cap front. Join the mitered corners by drilling pilot holes through the joints **(photo D)** and fastening them with glue and 2½" deck screws. Clamp the cap front and cap ends to the front of your worktable to hold them while you drive the screws. Fasten the cap back between the cap ends with 2½" wood screws, making sure the back edges are flush. Set the cap frame on the planter bin so the back edges are flush. Drill countersunk pilot holes, and drive 2½" deck screws through

the cap frame and into the side and end cleats.

MAKE THE TRELLIS. The trellis is made from pieces of 2 × 2 assembled in a crosshatch pattern. The exact number and placement of the 2 × 2 pieces is up to you—you can use the same spacing we used (see *Diagram*), or create your own. Cut the end posts (G), center post (H) and rails (I, J, K) to length. Lay the end posts and center post together side by side with their bottom edges flush, so you can gang-mark the rail positions. Use a square as a guide for drawing lines across all three posts, 18" up from the bottom. Draw the next line 7½" up from the first. Draw additional lines across the posts, spaced 7½" apart. Cut two 7"-wide scrap blocks, and use them to separate the posts as you assemble the trellis. Attach the rails to the posts in the sequence shown in the *Diagram*, using 2½" screws **(photo E)**. Alternate from the fronts to the backs of the posts when installing the rails.

APPLY FINISHING TOUCHES. Fasten the trellis to the back of the planter bin so the bottoms of the posts rest on the top edge of the base. Drive countersunk 2½" deck screws through the posts and into the cap frame. Install a 1"-dia. spade bit in your drill, and drill a pair of drainage holes in each board (see *Diagram*, page 105). Stain the finished project as desired. We used an exterior wood stain.

Temporary spacers hold the posts in position while the trellis crossrails are attached.

Driveway Marker

*An inviting yard ornament that graces the entrance to your driveway
or front walk, and directs foot traffic wherever you want it to go.*

CONSTRUCTION MATERIALS

Quantity	Lumber
1	2 × 4" × 8' cedar
1	2 × 2" × 6' cedar
2	1 × 6" × 8' cedar
4	1 × 2" × 8' cedar

Bestow a sense of order on your front yard by building this handsome cedar driveway marker. Position it on your lawn at the entry to your driveway to keep cars from wandering off the paved surface; or set a driveway marker on each side of your front walk to create a formal entry to your home.

This freestanding driveway marker has many benefits you'll appreciate: the fence-style slats slope away from the corner post to create a sense of flow; the broad corner post can be used to mount address numbers, making your home easier to find for visitors and in emergencies; and, behind the front slats, you'll find a spacious planter.

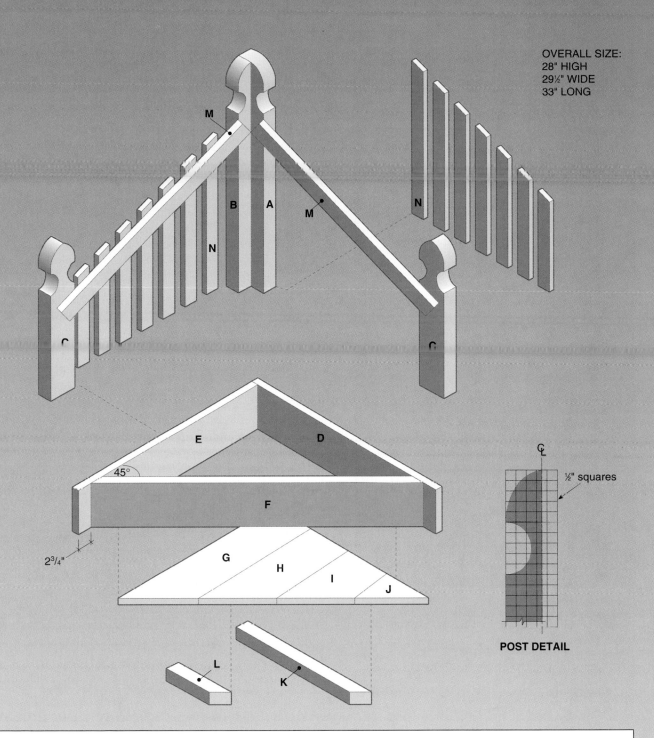

M

B   A

M

N

N

C

C

E   D

45°

F

2¾"

G

H

I

J

C̱L

½" squares

POST DETAIL

L

K

Cutting List

Key	Part	Dimension	Pcs.	Material
A	Corner post	1½ × 3½ × 28"	1	Cedar
B	Corner post	1½ × 1½ × 28"	1	Cedar
C	End post	1½ × 3½ × 18½"	2	Cedar
D	Planter side	⅞ × 5½ × 26½"	1	Cedar
E	Planter side	⅞ × 5½ × 25½"	1	Cedar
F	Planter back	⅞ × 5½ × 33"	1	Cedar
G	Bottom board	⅞ × 5½ × 23"	1	Cedar

Cutting List

Key	Part	Dimension	Pcs.	Material
H	Bottom board	⅞ × 5½ × 17"	1	Cedar
I	Bottom board	⅞ × 5½ × 11"	1	Cedar
J	Bottom board	⅞ × 5½ × 6"	1	Cedar
K	Long cleat	1½ × 1½ × 21"	1	Cedar
L	Short cleat	1½ × 1½ × 11"	1	Cedar
M	Stringer	⅞ × 1½ × 27"	2	Cedar
N	Slat	⅞ × 1½ × 20"	14	Cedar

Materials: Moisture-resistant glue, deck screws (¼", 2", 2½"), 2" brass numbers (optional), finishing materials.

Note: Measurements reflect the actual size of dimensional lumber.

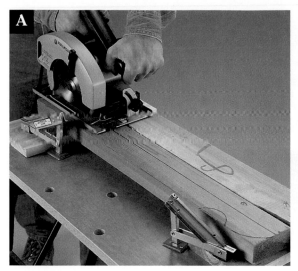

Rip the thin corner post to width with a circular saw.

Sand the top of the corner post assembly so the joint is smooth.

Lay the bin frame on the bottom boards and trace along the back inside edge to mark cutting lines.

Directions: Driveway Marker

CUT THE POSTS. This driveway marker is a freestanding yard ornament supported by single 2 × 4 posts at each end and a doubled 2 × 4 post at the corner. The tops of the posts feature French Gothic-style cutouts. Cut the corner posts (A, B) and end posts (C) to length from cedar 2 × 4. Draw a ½"-square grid pattern at the top of one of the end posts. Use the grid pattern on page 109 as a reference for drawing the top contour onto the end post.

Mark a centerpoint at the top of the post and draw the pattern as shown on one side. Reverse the pattern on the other side to create the finished shape. Use a jig saw to cut the end post to shape, then mount a drum sander attachment in your electric drill and use it to smooth out the cut. Use the shaped end post as a template to mark cutting lines at the top of the other end post. Cut and sand the other end post. To make the corner posts, mark centerpoints at the top of each corner post, then trace the contour of one end post on one side of the centerline. On one corner post, draw a line down the length of the post, 2" in from the side with no contour cutout—this will be the narrower post (B). To rip this post to width, first attach two pieces of scrap wood to your worksurface, then screw the post, facedown, to the wood scrap (making sure to drive screws in the waste area of the post). Next, butt a scrap the same thickness as the post next to the post, to use as a guide for the circular saw. Attach the guide board to the wood scraps, then set the edge

guide on the saw so it follows the outside edge of the scrap. Make the rip cut along the cutting line **(photo A).** Cut the contours at the tops of the corner posts, and sand smooth.

BUILD THE CORNER POST. The two corner post boards (A, B) are joined together to form a two-piece corner post. First, apply moisture-resistant wood glue to the ripped edge of the narrower post board (B), then lay it on the face of the wider post board (A) so the joint at the corner is flush and the tops of the contours come together in a smooth line. Drive 2½" deck screws through the wider board and into the edge of the narrower board, spaced at 4" intervals, and driven through countersunk pilot holes. After the glue sets, use a sander to smooth out the tops **(photo B).**

MAKE THE PLANTER FRAME. The planter is a triangular bin that fits in the back of the driveway marker. The bin includes a three-board frame that supports the bottom boards. Cut the planter sides (D, E) to length, making square cuts at the ends. The ends of the planter back (F) are beveled so they fit flush

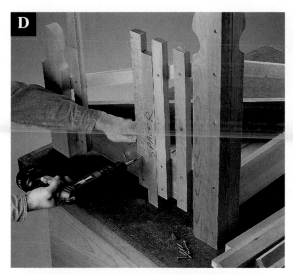

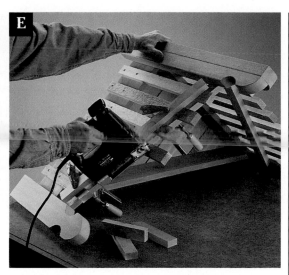

Use one slat as a spacer to set the correct gap as you fasten the slats to the bin and the stringers.

Use a cutting guide to trim the tops of the slats so they are flush with the tops of the stringers.

against the sides when the bin is formed. Set your circular saw to make a 45° cut, and cut the planter back to length, making sure the bevels both go inward from the same side (see *Diagram*). Apply glue to the ends of the planter back, then assemble the back and the sides by driving 2" deck screws through the outside faces of the side and into the ends of the back. This will create a setback of about 2¾" from the joints to the ends of the sides. Countersink the pilot holes slightly.

ATTACH THE BIN BOTTOM. Cut the bottom boards (G, H, I, J) to the full lengths indicated in the *Cutting List.* Lay the boards on your worksurface, arranged from shortest to longest, and butted together edge to edge. Set the bin frame on top of the boards so the inside edges of the frame sides are flush with the outer edges of the boards, and the bottom boards extend past the back edge of the frame. Trace along the inside of the frame back to mark cutting lines on the bottom boards **(photo C)**, and cut them with a circular saw.

Attach the bottom boards with glue and 2" deck screws driven through the frame and into the ends of the bottom boards. Make sure the bottoms of the bottom boards are flush with the bottom of the frame. Cut the long cleat (K) and short cleat (L) to size, making a 45° miter cut at one end of each cleat. Turn the planter bin upside down and attach the cleats so one is about 1½" from one of the sides, and the other is about 11½" from the same side—the cleats simply reinforce the bottom of the bin. Attach them by driving two 2" deck screws through each cleat where it meets each bottom board.

ATTACH THE BIN & POSTS. Set the bin on 2"-tall spacers, then fit the corner post assembly over the front corner of the bin and attach with glue and 1½" deck screws. Attach the end posts so each is 29½" away from the corner post assembly.

ATTACH STRINGERS & SLATS. The stringers (M) are attached between the tops of the posts to support the tops of the slats. Cut the stringers to size, and attach them to the insides of the

posts so the top edges are all 1½" below the bottom of the post contour at the point where the stringer meets each post. Next, cut all the slats (N) to 20" in length (the tops will be trimmed after the slats are installed). Attach them to the bin and the stringers, spaced at 1½" intervals—use one of the slats as a spacer to set the gap **(photo D).** Install all 14 slats, making sure the bottoms are flush with the bottom of the bin. Clamp a piece of 1 × 2 scrap against the outside faces of the slats to use as a cutting guide—the scrap should be directly opposite the stringer on the back side of the slats. Cut along the guide with a jig saw to trim the slats so the tops are slightly above the top of the stringer **(photo E).**

APPLY FINISHING TOUCHES. Sand all exposed surfaces and apply two or more coats of exterior wood stain. If your marker will be visible from the curb, you may want to attach 2"-high brass numbers to the corner post to indicate your street address.

PROJECT
POWER TOOLS

Backyard Fire Pit

*Bring backwoods intimacy into your backyard
with this raised campfire pit.*

You don't have to live at the beach or on a farm to enjoy the charm of an open campfire. In many areas, small open fires are allowed in backyards if you follow guidelines for size and notification.

This backyard campfire pit is an attractive structure that lets you build backyard campfires without scarring your backyard with a permanent fire pit. Because the concrete pavers that frame the pit area are loose-laid, they can be unstacked easily so you can move the fire pit out of the way when it is not in use. Two layers of cement-board serve as a firestop at the base of the pit. To build matching seating for your fire pit, see the plans for fire pit benches on pages 116 to 119.

NOTE: Regulations regarding open fires vary greatly. Check with your local Fire Department for policies and restrictions. One rule for open fires within city limits is that they can be no larger than 3' in diameter at the base, and must be at least 20' from a permanent structure. In some areas, you are required to notify Fire Department officials prior to building an open fire. Other restrictions may apply. Always use sound safety practices, and keep a fire extinguisher handy.

CONSTRUCTION MATERIALS

Quantity	Lumber
11	1 × 4" × 8' cedar
6	2 × 2" × 8' cedar
8	2 × 4" × 8' cedar
2	⅜" × 3 × 5' cementboard

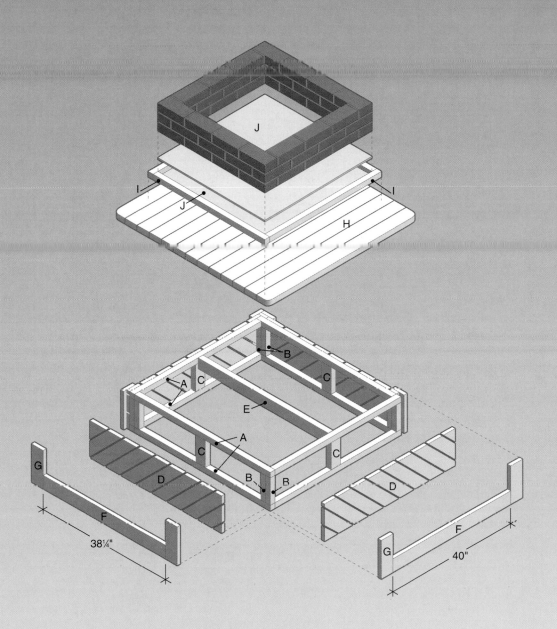

OVERALL SIZE:
13½" HIGH
49¾" WIDE
48" LONG

38¼"

40"

Cutting List						Cutting List				
Key	Part	Dimension	Pcs.	Material		Key	Part	Dimension	Pcs.	Material
A	Frame side	1½ × 1½ × 42"	8	Cedar		F	Bottom trim	⅞ × 3½ × *	4	Cedar
B	Frame end	1½ × 1½ × 7½"	8	Cedar		G	Side trim	⅞ × 3½ × 10½"	8	Cedar
C	Stud	1½ × 3½ × 7½"	4	Cedar		H	Deck slat	1½ × 3½ × 48"	13	Cedar
D	End slats	⅞ × 3½ × *	44	Cedar		I	Retainer	1½ × 1½ × 36"	4	Cedar
E	Joist	1½ × 3½ × 39"	1	Cedar		J	Firestop	⅝ × 34½ × 34½"	2	Cementboard

Materials: Galvanized deck screws (1½", 2½", 3½"), 3 × 8" concrete pavers (48).

Note: Measurements reflect the actual size of dimensional lumber.
*Cut to fit

113

Build four 2 × 2 frames, then join them together to make the large frame that supports the fire pit deck.

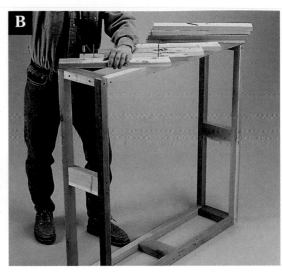

Fasten the slats to the frames with deck screws, using 16d nails for spacing between each end slat.

Directions: Backyard Fire Pit

BUILD THE FRAME. The frame sections are the first to be built on the fire pit. The slats, trim and joist are all attached to this supporting frame. Start by cutting the frame sides (A) and frame ends (B) to length from 2 × 2 cedar. Place the frame ends between the frame sides and fasten them with 2½" deck screws **(photo A).** Assemble the remaining frame ends and frame sides. Cut the studs (C) to length from 2 × 4 cedar and fasten them between the frame sides, centered between the frame ends. Fasten the frames together by driving 2½" deck screws through one frame end and into another.

FASTEN THE END SLATS. The cedar end slats are mounted diagonally on the frames and can be cut at an angle by using a circular saw and straightedge cutting guide (or a power miter box). Lay the frames on a flat surface and draw a 45° layout line across the frames, 3½" in from the frame corner. Next, cut the end slats (D) from 1 × 4

cedar and fasten them to the frames with 1½" deck screws, starting along the layout line and using 16d nails for spacing between each of the individual slats **(photo B).** Cut the slats in length so they overhang the frame edges by at least 1" on both ends. When all end slats are fastened to the frame, measure the precise end-slat overhang on each side of the frame and mark the overhang distance, two marks per frame side, on the top surfaces of the end slats. Draw a line around

the perimeter of each frame to connect the overhang marks on the end slats. Cut off the overhang on each frame side using a circular saw and a straightedge cutting guide **(photo C).** The cuts should be flush with the edges of the frame ends and sides. Be careful not to cut into the frame ends or sides, or into the deck screws fastening the end frames or end slats.

ATTACH THE JOIST & TRIM. Once the frame units have been assembled with end slats,

Cut off the slat overhang on each frame side using a circular saw and straightedge cutting guide.

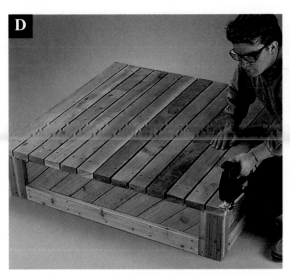

Cut roundover curves at the corners of the outside deck slats, using a jig saw.

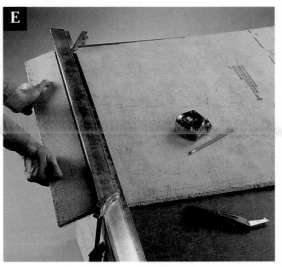

Cut cementboard to size by scoring and breaking to make the firestop.

the joist and trim are the next items to be fastened to the frames and slats. They provide structural support for the frame and a decorative cover for the end slats. Start by cutting the joist (E) to length from 2 × 4 cedar. Mount the joist between two of the studs, flush with the top edge of the frame side, using 3½" deck screws. Next, cut the bottom trim (F) and side trim (G) pieces to length from 1 × 4 cedar. Fasten them to the end slats around the perimeter of each frame with 1½" deck screws. Be sure to overlap the side trim, then cut the bottom trim to fit between the side trim pieces.

MAKE & ATTACH THE DECK SLATS. The deck slats tie the frame units together and provide a support surface for the fire pit. Cut the deck slats (H) to length from 2 × 4 cedar and position them on the frame and across the joist, leaving an equal overhang on all sides and ⁵⁄₁₆" spacing between the slats. Fasten the slats to the frame and joist with 2½" deck screws. Draw roundover lines with a 1½" radius on the out-

side deck slats, using a compass (or by tracing a 3"-dia. can). Cut the radius corners using a jig saw **(photo D)**, then smooth the rounded corners with a power sander.

DRY-SET THE PIT SURROUND. Before you make the parts for the pit, arrange your bricks or pavers in the pattern you plan to use for the pit surround. Because brick and paver sizes vary, the dimensions of the cementboard base and retainer frame may need to be adjusted to accommodate the finished dimensions of the surround. We used standard 3 × 8" concrete pavers (actual size is 2⅝" × 7⅝") to build the surround, which is reflected in the dimensions for the retainer and firestop that are listed in the *Cutting List* on page 113. However you stack the pavers or fire bricks, make sure the surround walls are at least 7" high, with an inside diameter of 3' or less.

BUILD THE RETAINER & FIRESTOP. Cut the retainers (I) to length from 2 × 2 cedar, using the adjusted length to fit your surround, if needed. Assemble the retainer strips into a

frame to wrap the surround, using 2½" deck screws. Measure the inside dimensions of the frame, and cut two pieces of ⅝"-thick cementboard to that size using a straightedge cutting guide and a sharp utility knife **(photo E)**.

APPLY FINISHING TOUCHES. Sand the fire pit, then apply exterior wood stain to all exposed surfaces. When the clear sealer has dried, center the retainer frame on the deck slats and place the layers of firestop into the retainer frame. Dry-lay your paver or brick surround walls inside the retainer frame, using the same pattern you dry-fit earlier. To move the backyard fire pit, or to clean the pit area, simply unstack the pavers or bricks.

Fire Pit Bench

Designed to match the Backyard Fire Pit shown on the previous pages, this versatile bench will be at home anywhere in your yard.

CONSTRUCTION MATERIALS

Quantity	Lumber
2	2 × 2" × 8' cedar
4	1 × 4" × 8' cedar
4	2 × 4" × 8' cedar
1	1 × 2" × 8' cedar

Summer cookouts, moon-lit bonfires or even a mid-winter warm-up are all perfect occasions to use this cedar fire pit bench, designed to accompany our Backyard Fire Pit (pages 112 to 115). If you are extremely ambitious, you can build four benches to surround the fire pit on all sides. If you don't need that much seating, build only two and arrange them to form a

cozy conversation area around the fire. Even without a fire pit, you can build a single bench as a stand-alone furnishing for your favorite spot in your yard or garden.

This solid cedar bench will seat up to three adults comfortably. The slats below give the bench strength, while providing a convenient spot for storing and drying firewood.

OVERALL SIZE:
18" HIGH
18½" WIDE
48" LONG

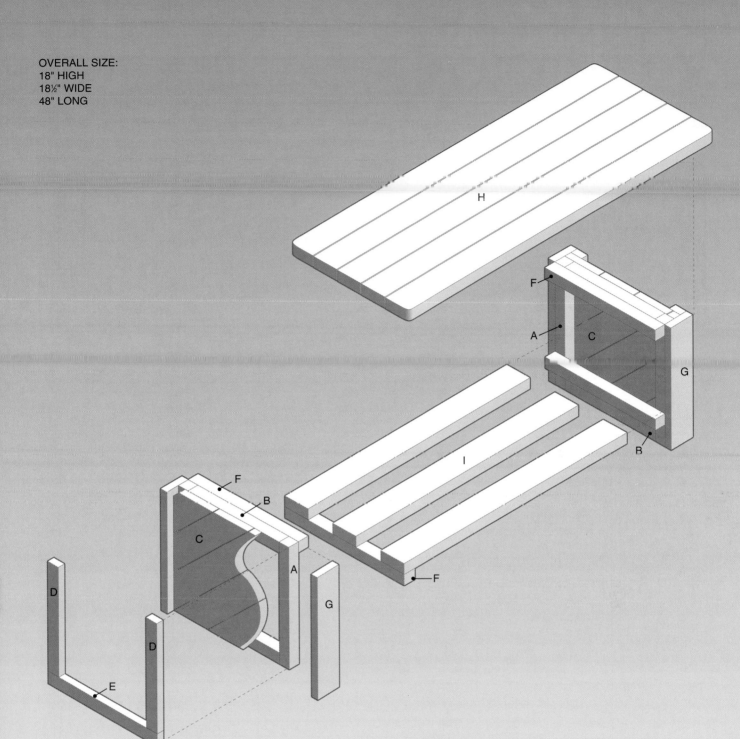

Cutting List

Key	Part	Dimension	Pcs.	Material
A	Frame side	1½ × 1½ × 16½"	4	Cedar
B	Frame end	1½ × 1½ × 14"	4	Cedar
C	End slat	⅞ × 3½ × *	12	Cedar
D	End trim	⅞ × 1½ × 15"	4	Cedar
E	Bottom trim	⅞ × 1½ × 17"	2	Cedar

Cutting List

Key	Part	Dimension	Pcs.	Material
F	Cleat	1½ × 1½ × 17"	4	Cedar
G	Side trim	⅞ × 3½ × 16½"	4	Cedar
H	Seat slat	1½ × 3½ × 48"	5	Cedar
I	Shelf slat	1½ × 3½ × 35"	3	Cedar

* Cut to fit

Materials: Galvanized deck screws (1½", 2½").

Note: Measurements reflect the actual size of dimensional lumber.

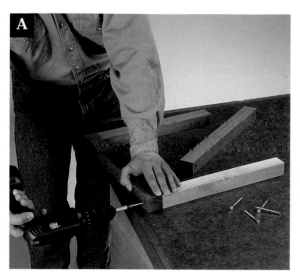

Fasten the frame sides to the frame ends with 2½" galvanized deck screws.

Trim off the ends of the slats so the ends are flush with the outside edges of the end frames.

Directions: Fire Pit Bench

BUILD THE END FRAMES. The seat slats are supported by 2 × 2 frames at the ends of the bench. To make the end frames, cut the frame sides (A) and frame ends (B) to length. Place a frame end between two frame sides, and fasten them together with 2½" deck screws driven through countersunk pilot holes in the frame sides and into the ends of the frame end **(photo A).** Attach another frame end between the free ends of the frame sides, then build the second end frame.

ATTACH THE END SLATS. The end slats are mounted at 45° angles to the end frames. The easiest way to cut the angles is to cut the slats so they over-hang the outsides of the frame, attach all the slats, then trim them flush with a single cut along each side. Start by laying the frames on a flat surface. Use a combination square as a guide for drawing a reference line at a 45° angle to one cor-ner on each frame, starting 3½" in from the corner. To measure and cut the end slats (C), lay

Use shelf slats to set the correct distance between the end-frame as-semblies, then attach the end frames to the bottoms of the seat slats.

the end of a full-length 1 × 4 cedar board across one frame so one edge meets the corner and the other edge follows the reference line. Position the board so the end overhangs the frame by an inch or two, then mark a point with an equal overhang on the other side of the frame. Cut the 1 × 4 at this point, then fasten the cut-off piece to the frame with pairs of 1½" deck screws driven into the

end frame. Lay the 1 × 4 back across the frame, butted up against the attached slat, and mark and cut another slat the same way. Attach the slat, and continue cutting and attaching the rest of the slats to cover the frame. Attach slats to the other end frame. Then, draw straight cutting lines on the tops of the slats, aligned with the outside edges of the end frames. Using a straightedge and a circular

Fasten the bottom cleats to the shelf slats, keeping the ends of the slats flush with the outside edges of the cleats.

Attach the bottom cleats to the end frames with deck screws. Use a spacer to keep the cleat 1½" up from the bottom of the bench.

saw, trim off the ends of the slats along the cutting lines **(photo B).**

COMPLETE THE END FRAMES. Cut the end trim (D) and bottom trim (E) pieces from 1 × 2 cedar, and fasten them to the outside faces of the end slats so they create a frame the same length and width as the end frame. Cut the side trim (G) pieces from 1 × 4 cedar and fasten to the frame assembly with

1½" deck screws, making sure the edges of the side trim are flush with the outside edges of the end frames and trim frames. Cut the cleats (F), and fasten a top cleat to the inside of each frame with 2½" deck screws. The top cleats should be flush with the tops of the end frames (the bottom cleats will be attached later).

ATTACH THE SEAT SLATS. Start by cutting the seat slats (H) to

length from 2 × 4 cedar. Lay the seat slats on a flat surface with the ends flush and ⅛" spaces between slats. Cut the shelf slats (I). Set the end frame assemblies on top of the seat slats, then slip two of the shelf slats between the ends to set the correct distance. Fasten the end-frame assemblies to the seat slats with 1½" deck screws driven through the cleats on the end frames **(photo C).**

ATTACH THE SHELF SLATS. Arrange the shelf slats on your worksurface so the ends are flush, with 1½" gaps between the slats. Lay the remaining two cleats across the ends of the slats, and fasten the cleats to the slats with 2½" deck screws **(photo D).** Set the shelf assembly between the ends of the bench, resting on a 1½" spacer. Attach the shelf by driving 2½" screws through the cleats and into the end frames **(photo E).**

APPLY FINISHING TOUCHES. Use a compass to draw a 1½"-radius roundover at the corners of the seat. Cut the roundovers with a jig saw. Sand the entire fire pit bench, paying special attention to the edges of the seat slats to eliminate any possibility of slivers—as an option, you can use a router with roundover bit to trim off the sharp edges. Apply exterior wood stain to all exposed surfaces (try to match the finish of the backyard fire pit, if you are building both pieces of the fire pit set).

TIP

When storing firewood, it is tempting to cover the wood with plastic tarps to keep it dry. But more often than not, tarps will only trap moisture and keep the firewood permanently damp. With good ventilation wood dries out quickly, so your best bet is to store it uncovered or in an open shelter.

Trash Can Corral

This two-sided structure keeps trash cans out of sight but accessible from the curb or alley.

CONSTRUCTION MATERIALS

Quantity	Lumber
3	2 × 4" × 6' cedar
2	2 × 2" × 10' cedar
1	1 × 8" × 6' cedar
7	1 × 6" × 10' cedar
8	1 × 4" × 8' cedar

Nothing can ruin a view from a favorite window like the sight of a dirty trash can—especially as garbage collection day draws near. With this trash can corral, you'll see a lovely, freestanding cedar fence instead of those unsightly garbage cans.

The two fence-style panels support one another, so you don't need to set fence posts in the ground or in concrete. And because the collars at the bases of the posts can be adjusted, you can position the can corral on uneven or slightly sloping ground. The staggered panel slats obstruct vision completely, but still allow air to pass through for much-needed ventilation.

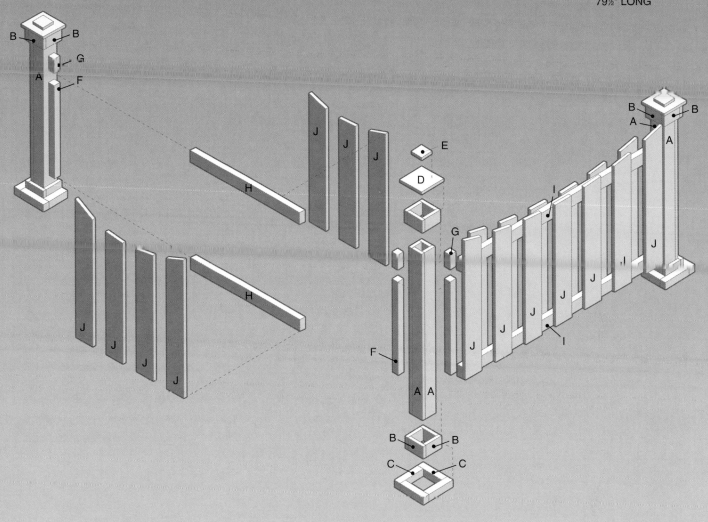

Cutting List

Key	Part	Dimension	Pcs.	Material
A	Post board	⅞ × 3½ × 48"	12	Cedar
B	Collar strip	⅞ × 3½ × 5¼"	24	Cedar
C	Foot strip	1½ × 1½ × 7½"	12	Cedar
D	Collar top	⅞ × 7¼ × 7¼"	3	Cedar
E	Collar cap	⅞ × 3½ × 3½"	3	Cedar

Cutting List

Key	Part	Dimension	Pcs.	Material
F	Long post cleat	1½ × 1½ × 26⅞"	4	Cedar
G	Short post cleat	1½ × 1½ × 4"	4	Cedar
H	Short stringer	1½ × 3½ × 35½"	2	Cedar
I	Long stringer	1½ × 3½ × 66"	2	Cedar
J	Slat	⅞ × 5½ × 40"	20	Cedar

Materials: Deck screws (1½", 2"), finishing materials.

Note: Measurements reflect the actual size of dimensional lumber.

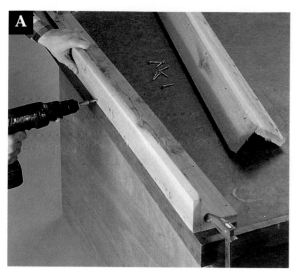

The post is made from four edge-joined boards.

Fit the top post collars onto each post and fasten them.

Attach the short post cleats 3⅝" up from the tops of the long post cleats. The top stringers on the panels fit between the cleats when installed.

Directions: Trash Can Corral

BUILD THE POSTS. Each post is made of four boards butted together to form a square. Cut the post boards (A) to length. After sanding the parts, clamp one post board on your work-surface, and butt another post board against it at a right angle. With the ends flush, attach the post boards with 2" deck screws, driven through counter-sunk pilot holes at 8" intervals **(photo A).** Repeat this process until all the post boards are fastened together in pairs, then fasten the pairs together to form the three posts.

MAKE & ATTACH THE COLLARS. Each post is wrapped at the top and bottom by a four-piece collar. The top collars each have a two-piece flat cap, and the base collars are wrapped with 1 × 2 strips for stability. Cut the collar strips (B), collar tops (D) and collar caps (E) to size. Join the collar strips together to form square frames, using 1½" deck screws. Center each collar cap on top of a collar top, and attach it with 1½" deck screws. Then, cover three of the frames with the tops and attach them with countersunk 1½" deck screws driven through the tops and into the top edges of the frames, completing the top collars. Slip a top collar over one end of each post, and drive countersunk, 1½" deck screws through the collars to secure them to the posts **(photo B).** Attach the three open frames to the other ends of the posts, with the bottom edges flush, then cut the foot strips (C) to length. Lay the foot strips together so they form

frames around the bottoms of the base collars, and screw them together with 2" deck screws. Make sure the bottoms of the frames are flush with the bottoms of the base collars, then attach the frames to the collars.

ATTACH THE CLEATS & SUPPORTS. The long and short post cleats (F, G) are attached to the posts to fit between and above the stringers that form the horizontal support for the corral panels. Cut the post cleats to length. Center a long post cleat side to side on one face of each post and attach it with 2" deck screws so the bottom of the cleat is 3½" above the top of the base collar on each post. On one of the posts, fasten another long post cleat on an adjacent post face, 4⅛" up from the bottom collar (this post will be the corner post). Center the short post cleats side to side on the same post faces as the long cleats, 3⅝" up from the tops of the long post cleats. Attach the short post cleats to the posts, making sure they are aligned with the long cleats **(photo C).**

Use 4½"-wide spacers to set the gaps between panel slats.

Use a flexible guide to mark the top contours.

BUILD THE FENCE PANELS. The two fence panels are built the same way. Start by cutting the short stringers (H), long stringers (I) and slats (J). Position the short stringers on your worksurface so they are parallel and separated by a 26⅞" gap. Attach a slat at both ends of the stringers, so the ends of the stringers are flush with the outside edges of the slats. Drive one 1½" deck screw through each slat and into the face of each stringer. Measure diagonally from corner to corner to make sure the fence panel is square. If the measurements are equal, the fence is square. If the measurements are not equal, apply pressure to one side of the square until they match. Drive another screw through each slat and into each stringer. Cut some 4½"-wide spacers to set the gaps between panel slats, and attach the remaining slats to the same side of the stringers with two screws driven at each joint. Make sure the bottoms of the slats stay aligned **(photo D).** Turn the panel over and attach slats to the other side, starting 4½" from the ends so the slats

are staggered on opposite sides of the stringers—there will only be three slats on this side. Build the long panel the same way.

CONTOUR THE PANEL TOPS. To lay out the curve at the top of each fence panel, you will need to make a marking guide. Cut a thin, flexible strip of wood to a length at least 6" longer than each fence panel. Tack nails at the top outside corner of each end slat, and tack another nail at the center of each panel (from side to side), ½" up from the top stringer. Position the flexible guides so the ends are above the nails at the ends of the panels, and the midpoints are below the nails in the centers of the panels, forming smooth curves in the flexible guides. Trace the contour created by each curve onto the tops of the slats **(photo E).** Cut the contours with a jig saw, using a blade short enough that it will not strike the slats on the other side. Repeat the steps on the other side of each panel—because of the thickness of the fence panels, you will need to mark and cut one side at a time. Sand the cuts smooth.

Set the completed fence panels between the cleats on the faces of the posts.

APPLY FINISHING TOUCHES. Position the fence panels between the posts so the top stringer in each panel fits in the gap between the long and short post cleats **(photo F).** Drive screws through the slats and into the cleats to fasten the panels to the posts. We applied exterior wood stain to protect the cedar. Set the trash can corral in your trash area. If need be, you can raise the height of any of the posts slightly by detaching the base collar, lifting the post, and re-attaching the collar.

Luminary

Dress up your yard or garden with these warm, decorative accents that look even better in bunches.

CONSTRUCTION MATERIALS

Quantity	Lumber
1	2 × 8 × *" cedar
1	1 × 2" × 8' cedar
1	1"-wide × 5' copper strip

*The shortest length available at most lumber yards is 6'. Since this is much more than you need for a single luminary, ask a yardworker if they have any scraps that are at least 6" long.

Luminaries are decorative outdoor accents that hold and protect candles or glass lamp chimneys. Traditionally, they are arranged in groups around an entrance or along a garden pathway. The simple slat-built luminary design shown here is easy and inexpensive to make. All you need are a few pieces of 1 × 2

cedar, some 1"-thick strips of copper and a 6"-dia. cedar base. The copper trim, glass chimneys and candles can be purchased at most craft stores. We used 22-gauge copper strips, which are thin enough to cut with scissors and will form easily around the luminary. Make sure to use copper nails to attach the strips.

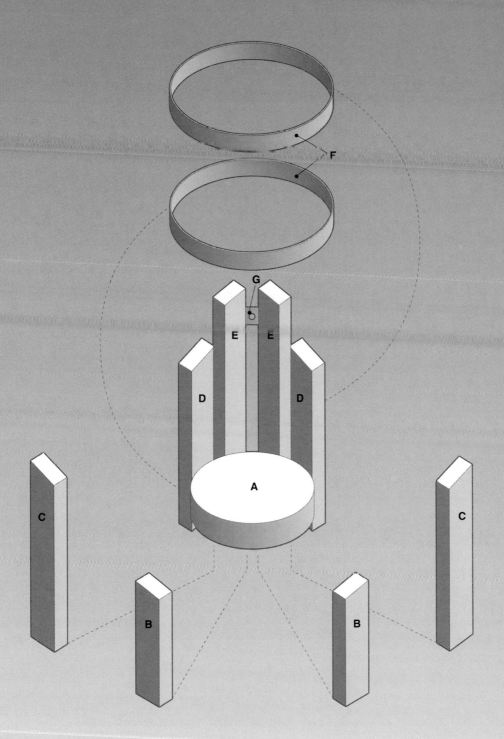

Cutting List

Key	Part	Dimension	Pcs.	Material
A	Base	1½ × 6 × 6"	1	Cedar
B	Front slat	⅞ × 1½ × 8"	2	Cedar
C	Short slat	⅞ × 1½ × 10"	2	Cedar
D	Middle slat	⅞ × 1½ × 12"	2	Cedar

Cutting List

Key	Part	Dimension	Pcs.	Material
E	Back slat	⅞ × 1½ × 14"	2	Cedar
F	Strap	1 × 25"	2	Copper
G	Hanger	1 × 3½"	1	Copper

Materials: 1⅝" deck screws, ¾" copper nails, candle and glass candle chimney.

Note: Measurements reflect the actual size of dimensional lumber.

Directions: Luminary

MAKE THE BASE. The base for the luminary is a round piece of cedar cut with a jig saw. Because the luminary slats are attached to the sides of the base, it is important that the base be as symmetrical and smooth as you can get it. Start by cutting the base (A) to 7¼" in length from a piece of 2 × 8 cedar (this will result in a square workpiece). Draw diagonal lines between opposite corners. The point where the lines intersect is the center of the board. Set the point of a compass at the centerpoint, and draw a 6"-dia., circular cutting line with the compass. Cut the base to shape along the cutting line, using a jig saw with a coarse-wood cutting blade (thicker blades are less likely to "wander" than thinner blades). Clamp a belt sander to your worksurface on its side, making sure the sanding belt is perpendicular to the worksurface. Sand the edges of the base to smooth out any rough spots, using the belt sander as a stationary grinder **(photo A).** If you are making more than one luminary, cut and sand all the bases at once for greater efficiency.

MAKE THE SLATS. The sides of each luminary are formed by four pairs of 1 × 2 cedar, cut to different lengths. All the slats are mitered on their top ends for a decorative effect that moves upward from front to back. Start by cutting the front slats (B), short slats (C), middle slats (D) and back slats (E) to length. On one slat, mark a

TIP

Prevent copper from oxidizing and turning green by coating it with spray-on polyurethane.

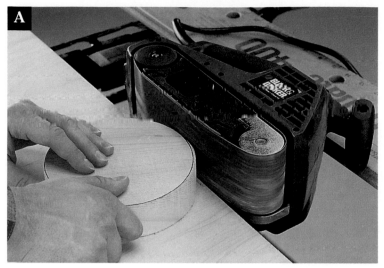

Smooth out the edges of the luminary base with a belt sander clamped to your worksurface.

Make a miter cut at the top of one slat, then use that slat as a guide for marking miter cuts on the rest of the slats.

point on one long edge, ½" in from an end. Draw a straight line from the point to the corner at the opposite edge. Cut along the line with a saw and miter box or with a power miter box. Using this slat as a guide, trace mitered cutting lines onto the tops of all the slats **(photo B).** Miter-cut the rest of the slats along the cutting lines.

ATTACH THE SLATS TO THE BASE. To attach the slats to the base, first drill a pair of ⅛"-dia. pilot holes at the bottom of

each slat. The pilot holes should be staggered to avoid splitting the base; drill one pilot hole ½" from the side and 1" up from the bottom; drill the other pilot hole ½" from the other side and 1½" up from the bottom. Countersink the pilot holes enough so the screw heads will be recessed. The slats should be installed so miters form a gradual upward slope from front to back (see *Diagram*, page 125). It is also important that the spacing between slats be exactly the same

Use ⅞"-wide spacers to maintain the gaps between the slats as you attach them to the base.

so that slats on opposite sides of the base are aligned. Use four ¾"-wide spacers to accomplish this. First, set the base on a ½"-thick block to create a recess. Then, arrange the four spacers in a stack so they form a hub over the center of the base (from above, the spacers should look like a pie cut into eight equal-sized pieces). Set the slats between the spacers so the bottoms are resting on the worksurface and they are flush against the base. Adjust the positions of the slats and spacers until each slat is opposite a slat across the base. Once you get the layout set, you may want to wrap a piece of masking tape around the slats, near the bottom, to hold them in place while you fasten them to the base. Now, carefully drive a 1⅝" deck screw through each pilot hole in each slat, and into the base **(photo C).** Do not overtighten the screws. Remove the spacers.

ATTACH THE STRAPS. We wrapped two 1"-wide straps made of 22-gauge (fairly light-weight) copper around the luminary to brace the slats. Try to find copper strips that are 25" long or longer at your local craft store. If you cannot find any strips that are that long, buy the shorter ones and splice them together with a 1" overlapping seam. Cut two 1"-wide copper strips to 25" in length to make the straps (F). Ordinary scissors will cut thin copper easily. Test-fit the straps by taping them in place around the slats. Mark drilling points for guide holes on the copper strap—one hole per slat, centered between the top and bottom of the strap. Drill ¹⁄₁₆"-dia. pilot holes through the drilling points, reposition the straps around the luminary (the bottom strap should conceal the screws heads at the bottoms of the slats). The second strap should be about 6¼" up from the bottom of the luminary. Insert a 6"-long block of wood between two slats that are opposite one another, then drive a ¾" copper nail through the pilot holes in those straps to secure them to the slats **(photo D).** Move the block, and drive copper nails through the rest of the pilot holes.

APPLY FINISHING TOUCHES. If you want to hang your luminary from a wall or post, cut a 1 × 3½"-long strip of copper to make a hanger (G). Drill a ⅜"-dia. hole through the center, then nail the hanger to the outsides of the back slats, about 1" down from the tops. To make a centering pin for holding a candle to the base, drive a 1¾" screw or a 6d nail up through the center of the base. Apply a coat of exterior wood stain if you plan to keep the luminary outdoors.

Brace the slats with a spacer as you tack on the copper strips.

Garden Bridge

*Whether it's positioned over a small ravine or a swirl of stones,
this handsome bridge will add romance and charm to your yard.*

CONSTRUCTION MATERIALS

Quantity	Lumber
4	4 × 4" × 8' cedar
2	2 × 10" × 8' cedar
10	2 × 4" × 8' cedar
2	1 × 8" × 8' cedar
2	1 × 3" × 8' cedar
8	1 × 2" × 8' cedar
2	½" × 2 × 8' cedar lattice

A bridge can be more than simply a way to get from point A to point B without getting your feet wet. This striking cedar footbridge will be a design centerpiece in any backyard or garden. Even if the nearest trickle of water is miles from your home, this garden bridge will give the impression that your property is graced with a tranquil brook, and you'll spend many pleasurable hours absorbing the peaceful images it inspires. You can fortify the illusion of flowing water by laying a "stream" of landscaping stones beneath this garden bridge. If you happen to have a small ravine or waterway through your yard, this sturdy bridge will take you across it neatly and in high style.

OVERALL SIZE:
46½" HIGH
38½" WIDE
97" LONG

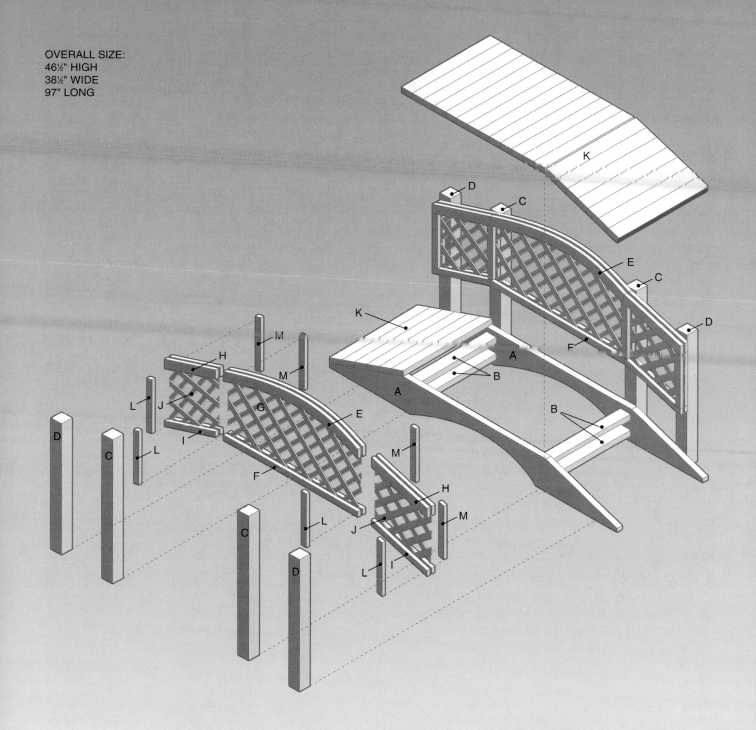

Cutting List				
Key	**Part**	**Dimension**	**Pcs.**	**Material**
A	Stringer	1½ × 9¼ × 96"	2	Cedar
B	Stretcher	1½ × 3½ × 27"	4	Cedar
C	Middle post	3½ × 3½ × 42"	4	Cedar
D	End post	3½ × 3½ × 38"	4	Cedar
E	Center handrail	⅞ × 7¼ × 44½"	4	Cedar
F	Center rail	⅞ × 1½ × 44½"	4	Cedar
G	Center panel	½ × 23½ × 44½"	2	Cedar lattice

Cutting List				
Key	**Part**	**Dimension**	**Pcs.**	**Material**
H	End handrail	⅞ × 2½ × 19½"	8	Cedar
I	End rail	⅞ × 1½ × 24"	8	Cedar
J	End panel	½ × 19 × 24"	4	Cedar lattice
K	Tread	1½ × 3½ × 30"	27	Cedar
L	Filler strip	⅞ × 1½ × 19"	8	Cedar
M	Trim strip	⅞ × 1½ × 20½"	8	Cedar

Materials: Lag screws (⅜ × 4"), deck screws (2", 3"), finishing materials.

Note: All measurements reflect the actual size of dimensional lumber.

Use a jig saw to make the arched cutouts in the bottoms of the 2 × 10 stringers.

Attach pairs of stretchers between the stringers with 3" deck screws.

Directions: Garden Bridge

MAKE THE STRINGERS. The first step in building the base involves cutting two long, heavy boards, called stringers (A), to shape. The stringers are the main structural members of the bridge. Both stringers have arcs cut into their bottom edges. The ends of the stringers are cut at a slant to create the gradual tread incline of the garden bridge. Start by cutting the stringers (A) to size. Before cutting the stringers to shape, carefully draw several guidelines on the workpieces: first, draw a centerline across the width of each stringer; then mark two more lines across the width of each stringer, 24" to the left and right of the centerline; finally, mark the ends of each stringer, 1" up from one long edge, and draw diagonal lines from these points to the top of each line to the left and right of the center. Use a circular saw to cut the ends of the stringers along the diagonal lines. Next, tack a nail on the centerline, 5¼" up from the bottom edge.

Cut the 4 × 4 posts to their finished height, then use lag screws to attach them to the outsides of the stringers.

Also tack nails along the bottom edge, 20½" to the left and right of the centerline. To lay out the arc at the bottom of each stringer, you will need to make a marking guide from a thin, flexible strip of scrap wood or plastic. Hook the middle of the marking guide over the center nail and slide the ends under the outside nails to form a smooth curve. Trace along the guide with a pencil to make the cutting line for the arc (you can mark both stringers this way, or mark and cut one, then use it as a template for marking the other). Remove the nails and marking guide, and cut the arcs on the bottom edge of each stringer with a jig saw **(photo A).**

Attach the treads to the stringers with 3" deck screws.

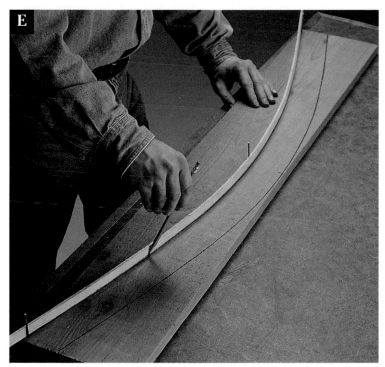

Use a flexible piece of plastic or wood as a marking guide when drawing the cutting lines for the center handrails.

tion the stretchers between them. Support the bottom stretchers with 1½"-thick spacer blocks for correct spacing. Fasten the stretchers between the stringers with countersunk 3" deck screws, driven through the stringers and into the ends of the stretchers. Turn the stringer assembly upside down, and attach the top stretchers **(photo B).** The footbridge will get quite heavy at this stage: you may want to build the rest of the project on-site. Clamp the middle posts to the outsides of the stringers so their outside edges are 24" from the center of the stringers. Make sure the middle posts are perpendicular to the stringers. Drill ¼"-dia. pilot holes through the stringers and into the middle posts. Attach the middle posts with ⅜"-dia. × 4"-long lag screws, driven through the stringers and into the posts **(photo C).** Clamp the end posts to the stringers, starting 7" from the stringer ends. Drill pilot holes and secure the end posts to the stringers with lag screws.

ATTACH THE TREADS. Cut the treads (K) to size. Position the treads on the stringers, making sure to space them evenly. The treads should be separated by gaps of about ¼". Test-fit all the treads before you begin installing them. Then, secure the treads with 3"-long countersunk deck screws **(photo D).**

ASSEMBLE THE BASE. Once the two stringers are cut to shape, they are connected with four straight boards, called stretchers (B), to form the base of the bridge. Posts that support the handrails are then attached to the base. These posts will also support the decorative lattice panel frames. Cut the stretchers (B), middle posts (C) and end posts (D) to size. Mark the stretcher locations on the insides of the stringers, 1½" from the top and bottom of the stringers. The outside edges of the stretchers should be 24" from the centers of the stringers (see *Diagram*, page 129), leaving the inside edges flush with the bottoms of the arcs. Stand the stringers upright and posi-

> **TIP**
>
> *Lattice panels need to be handled carefully, or they may fall apart. This is especially true when you are cutting the lattice panels. Before making any cuts, clamp two boards around the panel, close to the cutting line, to stabilize the lattice and protect it from the vibration of the saw. Always use a long, fine blade on your saw when cutting lattice.*

Use a jig saw to cut the panels and center handrails to shape.

Fasten 1 × 2 filler strips to the posts to close the gaps at the sides of the lattice panels.

ATTACH THE CENTER HAND-RAIL PANELS. The center panels are made by sandwiching lattice sections between 1 × 2 cedar frames. Each center panel has an arc along its top edge. This arc can be laid out with a flexible marking guide, using the same procedures used for the stringers. Once the center panels are made, they are attached to the inside faces of the middle posts. Start by cutting the center handrails (E), center rails (F) and center panels (G) to size. Using a flexible marking guide, trace an arc that begins 2½" up from one long edge of one center handrail. The top of this arc should touch the top edge of the workpiece. Lower the flexible marking guide 2½" down on the center handrails. Trace this lower arc, starting at the corners, to mark the finished center handrail shape **(photo E).** Using a jig saw, cut along the bottom arc. Trace the fin-

ished center handrail shapes onto the other workpieces, and cut along the bottom arc lines. Cut the center panels (G) to size from ½"-thick cedar lattice. Sandwich each center panel between a pair of center handrails so the top and side edges are flush. Clamp the parts, and gang-cut through the panel and center handrails along the top arc line with a jig saw **(photo F).** Unfasten the boards, and sand the curves smooth. Refasten the center panels between the arcs, ½" down from the tops of the arcs. Drive 2" deck screws through the inside center handrail and into the center panel and out-side center handrail. Drive one screw every 4 to 6"—be sure to use pilot holes and make an effort to drive screws through areas where the lattice strips cross, so the screws won't be visible from above. Fasten the center rails to the bottom of the center panels, flush with the

bottom edges. Center the panels between the middle posts, and fasten them to the posts so the tops of the handrails are flush with the inside corner of the middle posts at each end. The ends of the handrails are positioned at the center of the posts. Drive 3" deck screws through the center handrails and center rails to secure the panel to the center posts. Cut the filler strips (L) to size. The filler strips fit between the center handrails and center rails, bracing the panel and providing solid support for the loose ends of the lattice. Position the filler strips in the gaps between the center panels and the middle posts, and fasten them to the middle posts with 2" deck screws **(photo G).**

ATTACH THE END HANDRAIL PANELS. Like the center panels, the end panels are made by sandwiching cedar lattice sections between board frames and fastening them to posts.

Clamp the rough end panels to the posts at the ends of the bridge, and draw alignment markers so you can trim them to fit exactly.

The ends of the end panels and the joints between the end and center panels are covered by trim strips (M), which are attached with deck screws. This is the final step in building the garden bridge. Cut the end handrails (H), end rails (I) and end panels (J) to size. Position an end handrail and an end rail on your worksurface. Position an end panel over the pieces. Adjust the end handrail and end rail so the top of the panel is ½" down from the top edge of the end handrail. Sandwich the end panels between another set of end handrails and end rails, and attach the parts with 2" deck screws. Then clamp or hold the panels against the end posts and middle posts. Adjust the end panels so they are aligned with the center panel and the top inside corner of the end post. To cut the end panels to size, draw alignment marks near the end of the panel along the outside of the end

post **(photo H).** Unclamp the panels, and draw cutting lines connecting the alignment marks. Cut along the lines with a jig saw. Sand the end panels, and attach them to the posts with countersunk 3" deck screws, driven through the end

handrails and end rails. Slide filler strips between the end panels and the posts. Fasten the filler strips with 2" deck screws. Cut the trim strips (M) to size. Attach the trim strips over each joint between the end and center panels, and at the outside end of each end panel, with countersunk 3" deck screws **(photo I).**

APPLY FINISHING TOUCHES. Sand all the surfaces to smooth out any rough spots, and apply an exterior wood stain to protect the wood, if desired. You may want to consider leaving the cedar untreated, since that will cause the wood to turn gray—this aging effect may help the bridge blend better with other yard elements. Get some help, and position the bridge in your yard. For a dramatic effect, dig a narrow, meandering trench between two distinct points in your yard, line the trench with landscape fabric, then fill the trench with landscaping stones to simulate a brook.

Use deck screws to attach a trim strip over each joint between the end panels and center panels.

Fold-up Lawn Seat

With this fold-up seat built for two, you don't have to sacrifice comfort and style for portability.

CONSTRUCTION MATERIALS

Quantity	Lumber
1	2 × 8" × 6' cedar
4	2 × 4" × 8' cedar
2	1 × 6" × 8' cedar

Even though this cedar lawn seat folds up for easy transport and storage, it is sturdier and more attractive than just about any outdoor seating you are likely to make or buy. The backrest and legs lock into place when the seat is in use. To move or store this two-person seat, simply fold the backrest down and tuck the legs into the seat

frame to convert the seat into a compact package.

Because it is portable and stores in a small space, you can keep the fold-up lawn seat tucked away in a garage or basement and set it up for extra seating when you are entertaining. Or, if security around your home is an issue, you can bring it inside easily during times when you're not home.

OVERALL SIZE:
34⅛" HIGH
20" DEEP
42" LONG

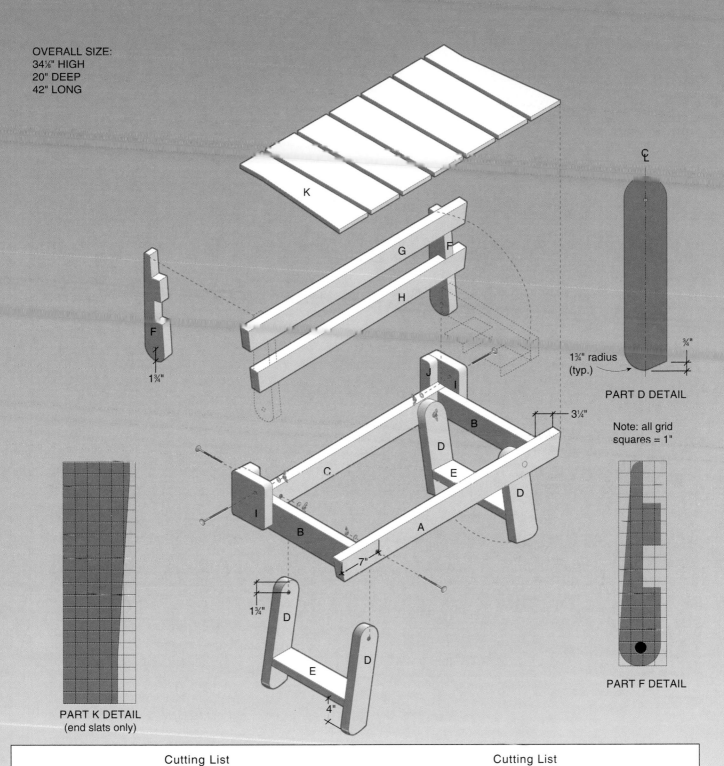

PART D DETAIL

1¾" radius
(typ.)

Note: all grid
squares = 1"

PART F DETAIL

PART K DETAIL
(end slats only)

Cutting List				
Key	Part	Dimension	Pcs.	Material
A	Front seat rail	1½ × 3½ × 42"	1	Cedar
B	Side seat rail	1½ × 3½ × 17"	2	Cedar
C	Back seat rail	1½ × 3½ × 35½"	1	Cedar
D	Leg	1½ × 3½ × 16¼"	4	Cedar
E	Stretcher	1½ × 3½ × 13⅞"	2	Cedar
F	Backrest post	1½ × 3½ × 17"	2	Cedar

Cutting List				
Key	Part	Dimension	Pcs.	Material
G	Top rest	1½ × 3½ × 42"	1	Cedar
H	Bottom rest	1½ × 3½ × 40"	1	Cedar
I	Cleat	1½ × 7¼ × 6"	2	Cedar
J	Stop	1½ × 7¼ × 2"	2	Cedar
K	Slat	⅞ × 5½ × 20"	7	Cedar

Materials: Moisture-resistant glue, ⅜ × 4" carriage bolts (6) with washers and wing nuts, deck screws (1¼", 2", 2½").

Note: Measurements reflect the actual size of dimensional lumber.

135

Directions:
Fold-up Lawn Seat

MAKE THE LEGS. The lawn seat is supported by two H-shaped legs that fold up inside the seat. Start by cutting the legs (D) to the length shown in the *Cutting List* on page 135. Mark a point 1¾" in from one end of each leg, centered side to side. Set the point of a compass at each point and draw a 1¾"-radius semicircle to make cutting lines for roundovers at the ends of the legs (these ends will be the tops of the legs). Then, drill a ⅜"-dia. guide hole through each point. At the other end of each leg, mark a centerpoint measured from side to side. Measure in ¾" from the end along one edge, and mark another point. Connect

Fasten the stretchers between the legs with glue and deck screws.

Smooth out the post notches with a wood file.

the points with a straight line, and cut along the line with a jig saw to create the flat leg bottoms that will contact the ground. Then mark 1¾"-radius roundovers at the opposite edges of the leg bottoms. Cut the roundovers with a jig saw. Cut the stretchers (E) to length. Attach one stretcher between each pair of legs so the bottoms of the stretchers are 4" up from the bottoms of the legs **(photo A).** Use moisture-resistant wood glue and 2½" deck screws driven through countersunk pilot holes to attach the stretchers, making sure the flat ends of the legs are on the same side of the stretcher.

MAKE THE BACKREST POSTS. Two posts are notched to hold the two boards that form the backrest. Cut the backrest posts (F) to size. On one edge of each post, mark points 6½", 10" and 13½" up from the end of the post. Draw a line lengthwise on each post, 1½" in from the edge with the marks. Extend lines out from each point so they cross the lengthwise line. This will create the outlines for cutting notches in the post (see *Diagram*, page 63). Use a jig saw cut out the notches, then file or sand the cuts smooth **(photo B).** Use a compass to draw a semicircle with a 1¾" radius at the bottom of each post. Measure up 1¾" from the bottoms, and mark drilling points that are centered side to side. Drill a ⅜"-dia. guide hole through each drilling point to complete the posts. Using the *Part F Details* as a guide, mark the 1" tapers on the back edges of the posts. Make these cuts with a jig saw, then sand the posts smooth. Sand a little extra off the top to dull any

sharp edges.

ASSEMBLE THE BACKREST. Cut the top rest (G) and bottom rest (H). Mark trim lines at both ends of each board, starting ½" in from the ends on one edge and tapering to the opposite corner. Trim off the ends along these lines with a jig saw. Position the posts on their back (tapered) edges, and insert the top and bottom rests into their notches. Position the posts 32½" apart. Center the rests on the posts so the overhang is equal on each rest, and attach the rests to the posts with glue and 2" deck screws **(photo C).**

BUILD THE SEAT FRAME. The seat frame is made by attaching two side rails between a front rail and back rail. The front rail is tapered to match the backrest. Start by cutting the front seat rail (A), side seat rails (B) and back seat rail (C) to length. Sand the parts to smooth out any rough edges. Drill a pair of evenly spaced, countersunk pilot holes for 2½" deck screws, 4" in from each end of the front rail to attach the side rails, then drill centered, ⅜"-dia. holes, 7" in from each end for the leg assemblies. Also drill ⅜"-dia. pilot holes for carriage bolts through the back rail, centered 3¾" in from each end. Make a ½" taper cut at each end of the front rail. Apply moisture-resistant glue to one end of each side rail, and position the side rails against the front rails. Fasten the side rails to the back of the front rail by driving deck screws through the pilot holes and into the ends of the side rails. Fasten the back rail to the free ends of the side rails with glue and screws. Make sure the ends are flush. Sand the frame to round over the bottom, outside edges.

Center the top and bottom rests in the post notches, and fasten them with glue and deck screws.

Attach the cleats and stops to the rear edges of the seat frame.

JOIN THE LEGS & SEAT FRAME. Position the leg assemblies inside the seat frames, making sure the rounded corners face the ends of the frame. Apply paste wax to four carriage bolts. Align the guide holes in the legs and seat frame, then attach the parts with the carriage bolts (see *Diagram*).

ATTACH THE CLEATS & STOP. The cleats (I) and stops (J) are attached to each other on the back corner of the seat frame to provide an anchor for the backrest. Once the cleats and stops are attached, carriage bolts are driven through the cleats and into the posts on the backrest. Cut the cleats and stops to size. The stops fit flush against the back edges of the cleats. As its name suggests, the stop supports the backrest and prevents it from folding all the way over when you sit on the chair. Position a stop against a cleat face, flush with one long edge. Make sure the top and bottom edges are flush, and attach the stop to the cleat with glue and 2½" deck screws. Drill a ⅜"-dia. hole through each cleat, centered 1¾" in from the front and top edges. Smooth the edges of the cleats and stops with a sander, and attach them to the rear corners of the seat frame with glue and 2½" deck screws **(photo D).** Make sure the bottom edges of the cleats and stops are ½" up from the bottom of the frame.

ATTACH THE SEAT SLATS. The seat slats are all the same length, but the end slats are tapered from front to back. Cut the slats (K), then plot out a 1"-grid pattern onto two of the slats. Use the *Part K Detail* as a guide for drawing cutting lines at the edges of the two slats (note that the taper straightens out 4" from the back of the slat). Cut the tapers with a circular saw or jig saw. Smooth out all the edges of all the seat slats with a router and roundover bit, or with a sander, then attach the slats to the seat frame. Make sure the wide ends of the end slats are flush with the ends of the frame, and the back ends of all slats are flush with the back edge of the frame. The gaps between slats should be equal. Use glue and

Attach the backrest to the seat frame with carriage bolts and wing nuts.

1¼" screws to secure the slats.

ASSEMBLE THE LAWN SEAT. Finish all the parts with an exterior wood stain. Fit the backrest assembly between the cleats. Align the carriage bolt holes in the posts and cleats, and insert the bolts. Add washers and wing nuts to the free ends to secure the backrest to the seat frame **(photo E).** Hand-tighten the wing nuts to lock the backrest and legs in position. Loosen the wing nuts when you want to fold up the lawn seat for transport or storage.

Gardener's Tote

*Organize and transport your essential gardening supplies
with this handy cedar tote box.*

CONSTRUCTION MATERIALS

Quantity	Lumber
1	1 × 10" × 6' cedar
1	1 × 6" × 6' cedar
1	1 × 4" × 6' cedar
1	1 × 2" × 6' cedar

This compact carrying tote has plenty of room and is a real blessing for gardeners. With special compartments sized for seed packages, spray cans and hand tools, it is a quick and easy way to keep all your most-needed supplies organized and ready to go. The bottom shelf is well suited for storing kneeling pads or towels. The gentle curves cut into the sides of the storage compartment make access easy and provide a nice decorative touch. The sturdy cedar handle has a comfortable hand-grip cutout. You'll find this tote to be an indispensible gardening companion, whether you're tending a small flower patch or a sprawling vegetable garden.

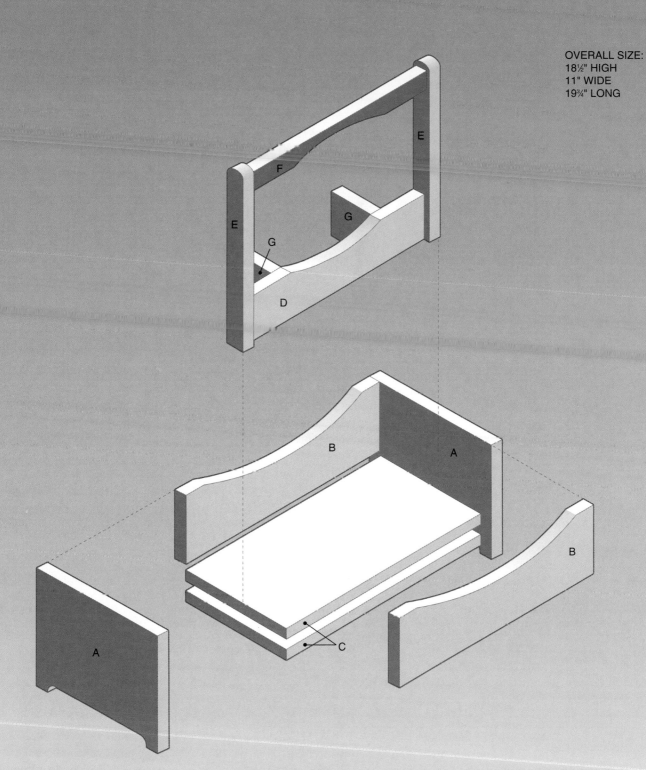

OVERALL SIZE:
18½" HIGH
11" WIDE
19¾" LONG

Key	Part	Cutting List		
		Dimension	Pcs.	Material
A	End	⅞ × 9¼ × 11"	2	Cedar
B	Side	⅞ × 5½ × 18"	2	Cedar
C	Shelf	⅞ × 9¼ × 18"	2	Cedar
D	Divider	⅞ × 3½ × 16¼"	1	Cedar

Key	Part	Cutting List		
		Dimension	Pcs.	Material
E	Post	⅞ × 1½ × 14"	2	Cedar
F	Handle	⅞ × 1½ × 16¼"	1	Cedar
G	Partition	⅞ × 3½ × 3⅞"	2	Cedar

Materials: Moisture-resistant glue, deck screws (1¼, 2"), finishing materials.

Note: Measurements reflect the actual size of dimensional lumber.

139

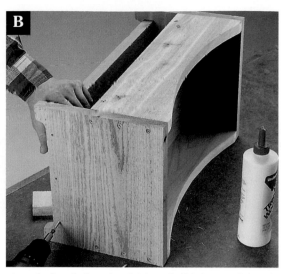

Use a jig saw to cut the curves on the bottom edge of each end, forming feet for the box.

Attach the shelves by driving deck screws through the ends and into the shelf ends.

Directions:
Gardener's Tote

BUILD THE BOX. The gardener's tote is essentially a wooden box with a handle and a storage shelf beneath the bottom of the box. The sides of the box have curved cutouts to improve access, and the ends have scalloped cutouts to create feet, making the tote more stable. Start by cutting the ends (A), sides (B) and shelves (C) to size. Sand all parts with medium-grit sandpaper to smooth out any rough edges after cutting. On one side, mark points on one long edge, ½" in from the ends. Mark another point, ½" down from the center of the same long edge. Draw a graceful curve connecting those points, forming the cutting line for the curve at the top. Cut the curve with a jig saw, and sand it to remove any rough spots. Position this completed side piece on the uncut side piece, so their edges and ends are flush. Trace the curve onto the uncut side, and cut that side piece to match the first. Clamp the sides together,

and gang-sand both curves to smooth out any rough spots. To cut the curves on the bottom edges of the ends, first use a compass to draw ¾"-radius semicircles, with the centerpoint 1¾" from each end. These semicircles form the rounded end of each scalloped cutout. Using a straightedge, draw a straight line connecting the tops of the circles, completing the cutout shape. Cut the curves with a jig saw **(photo A),** and sand the ends to remove any saw marks or other rough spots. To attach the ends to the sides, drill pilot holes for countersunk 2" deck screws at each end, ⁷⁄₁₆" in from the edges. Position the pilot holes 1", 3" and 5" down from the tops of the ends. Apply glue to the ends of the sides, and fasten them to the ends with deck screws, driven through the ends and into the sides. Make sure the top and outside edges are flush. Mark the shelf locations on the inside faces of the ends; the bottom of the lower shelf is ¾" up from the bottoms of the ends, and the upper shelf position is 3¾" up from the

bottoms of the ends. Drill pilot holes for 2" deck screws ⁷⁄₁₆" up from the lines. Apply glue to the shelf ends, and position them between the ends with their bottom edges on the lines. Drive 2" deck screws through the ends and into the shelves **(photo B)** to attach the parts.

BUILD THE DIVIDER ASSEMBLY. The internal sections of the gardener's tote are made as a separate assembly and then inserted into the box. Start by cutting the divider (D), posts (E), handle (F) and partitions (G) to size. Use a sander or a jig saw to make a ⅜" roundover on the corners of one end of each post. The divider and handle have shallow arcs cut on one long edge. Draw the arcs on the handle and divider. First, mark points 4" in from each end; then, mark a centered point, ⅝" up from one long edge on the handle. On the divider, mark a centered point ⅝" down from one long edge. Draw a graceful curve to connect the points, and cut along the cutting lines with a jig saw. Sand all the edges of the handle and divider. Drill two counter-

Drill countersunk pilot holes through the posts before you attach them to the handle.

sunk pilot holes on the divider to attach the partitions. Center the pilot holes $\frac{7}{16}$" to each side of the curve. Use moisture-resistant glue and 2" deck screws, driven through the divider and into the partition edges, to attach the partitions to the divider. Clamp the posts together with their ends flush, and mark a $3\frac{1}{2}$"-long reference line on each post, $\frac{7}{8}$" in from the joint formed when the parts are clamped together—start the reference lines at the square post ends. Connect the lines at the tops to indicate the position of the divider ends. Drill two countersunk pilot holes through the posts, centered between each reference line and the inside edge **(photo C).** Next, drill two countersunk pilot holes in each post, centered $\frac{1}{2}$" and 1" down from the top ends. Position the divider between the posts, aligned with the pilot holes. One face of the divider should be flush with a post edge. Fasten the handle and divider between the posts with moisture-resistant glue and 2" deck screws. Set the assembly

into the box to make sure it fits.

INSTALL THE DIVIDER. Make sure the partitions fit squarely against the sides. Trace post position lines on the ends **(photo D).** Apply glue to the ends where the posts will be fastened. Attach the posts to the ends with countersunk $1\frac{1}{4}$ deck screws, driven through the posts and into the ends. Drive two evenly spaced coun-

tersunk 2" screws through the sides and into each outside partition end.

APPLY THE FINISHING TOUCHES. Sand all the surfaces with medium (100- or 120-grit) sandpaper to smooth out any rough spots, then finish-sand with fine (150- or 180-grit) sandpaper. If you want to preserve the cedar tones, apply exterior wood stain to all the surfaces of the gardener's tote. But you may prefer to simply leave the wood uncoated for a more rustic appearance: as you use the tote, it will slowly turn gray.

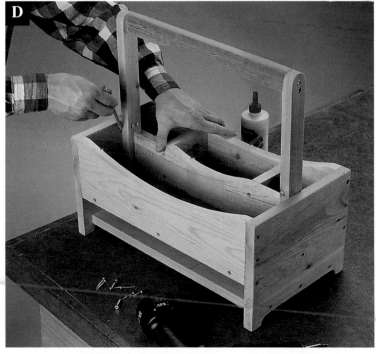

Draw reference lines for the post position on the box ends.

Plant Boxes

*Build these simple plant boxes in whichever
size or amount best meets your needs.*

CONSTRUCTION MATERIALS*

Quantity	Lumber
3	1 × 2" × 8' cedar
6	1 × 4" × 8' cedar
1	⅜" × 4 × 8' fir siding
1	¾" × 2 × 4' CDX plywood

*To build all three plant boxes as shown

Planters and plant boxes come in a vast array of sizes and styles, and there is a good reason for that: everyone's needs are different. So rather than build just one planter that may or may not work for you, we've come up with a planter design that is easy to change to fit your space and planting demands.

We've included measurements for building this plant box in three sizes and shapes: short and broad for flowers or container plants; medium for spices and herbs or small trees and shrubs; and tall and narrow for vegetables or flowering vines that will cascade over the cedar surfaces. The three boxes are proportional to one another, so you can build all three and arrange them in a variety of patterns, including the tiered effect shown above.

142

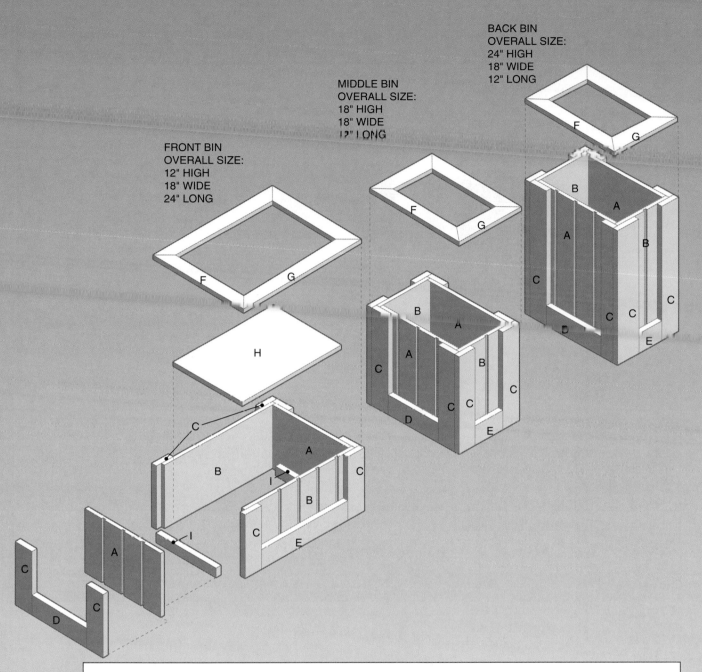

BACK BIN
OVERALL SIZE:
24" HIGH
18" WIDE
12" LONG

MIDDLE BIN
OVERALL SIZE:
18" HIGH
18" WIDE
12" LONG

FRONT BIN
OVERALL SIZE:
12" HIGH
18" WIDE
24" LONG

		Cutting List						
Key	Part	Front Bin Dimension	Pcs.	Middle Bin Dimension	Pcs.	Back Bin Dimension	Pcs.	Material
A	End panel	⅝ × 15 × 11⅛"	2	⅝ × 15 × 17⅛"	2	⅝ × 15 × 23⅛"	2	Siding
B	Side panel	⅝ × 22¼ × 11⅛"	2	⅝ × 10¼ × 17⅛"	2	⅝ × 10¼ × 23⅛"	2	Siding
C	Corner trim	⅞ × 3½ × 11⅛"	8	⅞ × 3½ × 17⅛"	8	⅞ × 3½ × 23⅛"	8	Cedar
D	Bottom trim	⅞ × 3½ × 9¼"	2	⅞ × 3½ × 9¼"	2	⅞ × 3½ × 9¼"	2	Cedar
E	Bottom trim	⅞ × 3½ × 15¼"	2	⅞ × 3½ × 3¼"	2	⅞ × 3½ × 3¼"	2	Cedar
F	Top cap	⅞ × 1½ × 18"	2	⅞ × 1½ × 18"	2	⅞ × 1½ × 18"	2	Cedar
G	Top cap	⅞ × 1½ × 24"	2	⅞ × 1½ × 12"	2	⅞ × 1½ × 12"	2	Cedar
H	Bottom panel	¾ × 16 × 19½"	1	¾ × 16 × 7½"	1	¾ × 16 × 7½"	1	Plywood
I	Cleat	⅞ × 1½ × 12"	2	⅞ × 1½ × 12"	2	⅞ × 1½ × 12"	2	Cedar

Materials: Deck screws (1¼", 1½", 3"), 6d galvanized finish nails, and finishing materials.

Note: Measurements reflect the actual thickness of dimensional lumber.

Directions: Plant Boxes

Whatever the size of the plant box or boxes you are building, use the same basic steps for construction. The only difference between the boxes is that the size of some of the components varies from box to box. If you need larger, smaller, broader or taller plant boxes than those shown, it's a fairly easy process to create your own cutting list based on the *Diagram* and dimensions shown on page 143. If you are creating your own dimensions, it is definitely worth your time to double- or triple-check the new part sizes on paper before you actually start to cut the wood. If you are building several planters, do some planning and sketching to make the most efficient use of your wood and to save time by gang-cutting parts that are the same size and shape.

MAKE & ASSEMBLE THE BOX PANELS. The end and side panels are simply rectangular pieces of sheet siding fastened together with galvanized deck screws. We used fir sheet siding with 4"-on-center grooves for a decorative look, but you can substitute any exterior-rated sheet goods (or even dimensional lumber) to match the

Cut the end panels and side panels to size using a circular saw and a straightedge cutting guide.

rest of your yard or home. Start the project by cutting the end panels (A) and side panels (B) to size from ⅝"-thick fir sheet siding using a circular saw and straightedge cutting guide **(photo A).** Lay an end panel face-side-down on a flat work-surface and butt a side panel, face-side-out, up to the end of the end panel. Fasten the side panel to the end panel with 1½" deck screws. Position the second side panel at the other end of the end panel and fasten it with deck screws. Lay the remaining end panel face-side-down on the worksurface. Position the side panel assembly over the end panel, placing the end panel between the side panels and keeping the edges of the side panels flush with the edges of the end panel. Fasten the side panels to the end panel with deck screws. Countersink all screws slightly so the heads are below the surface of the wood.

ATTACH THE TRIM. The cedar trim serves not only as a decorative element, but also as a structural reinforcement to the side panels. Begin the trim in-

stallation by cutting the corner trim (C) to length from 1 × 4 cedar (most cedar has a rough texture on one side; we chose to install our trim pieces with the rough side facing out for a more rustic look, but if you want a more finished appearance, install the pieces with the smooth side facing out). Overlap the edges of the corner trim pieces at the corners to create a square butt joint. Fasten the corner trim pieces directly to the panels with 1¼" deck screws driven through the inside faces of the panels and into the corner trim pieces **(photo B).** For additional support, drive screws or galvanized finish nails through the overlapping corner trim pieces and into the edges of the adjacent trim piece (this is called "lock-nailing"). Next, cut the bottom trim pieces (D, E) to length from 1 × 4 cedar and fasten the pieces to the end and side panels, between the corner trim pieces. Use 1¼" deck screws driven through the side and end panels and into the bottom trim pieces.

Fasten the corner trim to the panels by driving deck screws through the panels into the trim.

INSTALL THE TOP CAPS. The top caps fit around the top of the plant box to create a thin ledge that keeps water from seeping into the end grain of the panels and trim pieces (with the mitered corners, the top caps also add a nice decorative touch). Cut the top caps (F, G) to length from 1 × 2 cedar. Cut 45° miters at both ends of one cap piece, using a power miter saw or a miter box and backsaw. Tack the mitered cap piece to the top edge of the planter, keeping the outside edges flush with the outer edges of the corner trim pieces. To be assured of a proper fit, use this cap piece as a guide for marking and cutting the miters on the rest of the cap pieces. Miter both ends of each piece, then tack it to the box so it makes a square corner with the previously installed piece. If the corners do not work out exactly right, you can loosen the pieces and adjust the arrangement until everything is as square as it can get. Then permanently fasten all the cap pieces to the box with 6d galvanized finish nails.

INSTALL THE BOX BOTTOM. The bottom of the planter box is supported by 1 × 2 cleats (I) that are fastened inside the box, flush with the bottoms of the side and end panels. Cut the cleats to size and screw them to the end panels with 1½" deck screws **(photo C).** On the taller bins you may want to mount the cleats higher on the panels so the box won't need as much soil when filled, but if you choose to do this, add cleats on the side panels for ex-tra support. Cut the bottom panel (H) to size from ¾"-thick exterior-rated plywood (we used CDX plywood). Set the bottom panel onto the cleats (you do not need to use any fasteners to hold it in place).

APPLY FINISHING TOUCHES. After you've built all the boxes, sand all the edges and surfaces to remove rough spots and splinters. Apply two or three coats of exterior wood stain to all the surfaces to protect the wood. When the finish has dried, fill the boxes with potting soil. Or, if you are using shorter boxes, you may prefer to simply place potted plants inside the planter box.

Attach 1 × 2 cleats to the inside faces of the box ends to support the bottom panel.

Compost Bin

*Convert yard waste to garden fertilizer inside this
simple and stylish cedar compost bin.*

CONSTRUCTION MATERIALS

Quantity	Lumber
4	4 × 4" × 4' cedar post
5	2 × 2" × 8' cedar
8	1 × 6" × 8' cedar fence boards

Composting yard debris is an increasingly popular practice that makes good environmental sense. Composting is the process of converting organic waste into rich fertilizer for the soil, usually in a compost bin. A well-designed compost bin has a few key features: it's big enough to contain the organic material as it decomposes; it allows cross-flow of air to speed along the process; and the bin area is easy to access for adding waste, turning the decomposing compost, and removing the fully composted material. This compost bin has all these features, plus one additional benefit not shared by most compost bins: it is very attractive.

146

OVERALL SIZE:
30" HIGH
40½" WIDE
48" LONG

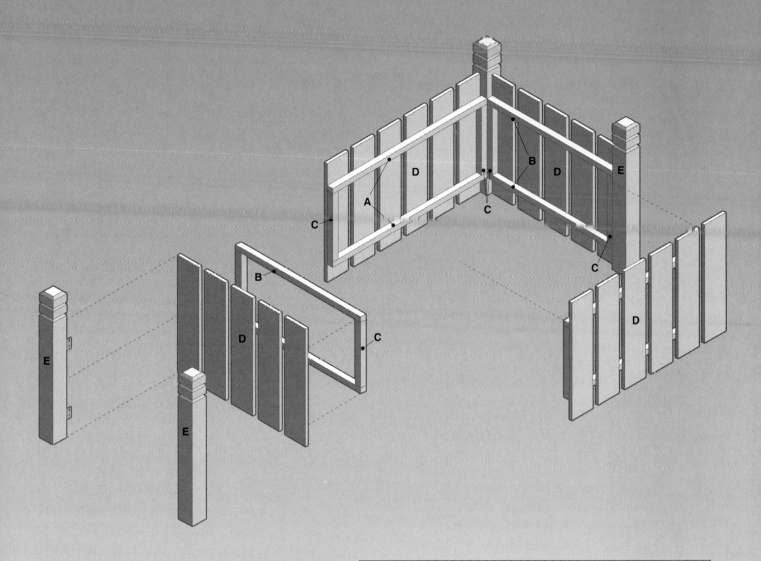

Cutting List				
Key	**Part**	**Dimension**	**Pcs.**	**Material**
A	End rail	1½ × 1½ × 41"	4	Cedar
B	Side rail	1½ × 1½ × 33½"	4	Cedar
C	Cleat	1½ × 1½ × 15"	8	Cedar
D	Slat	¾ × 5½ × 27"	22	Cedar
E	Post	3½ × 3½ × 30"	4	Cedar

Materials: Galvanized deck screws (2" and 3"), hook-and-eye latch mechanism, 3 × 3" brass butt hinges (one pair) and screws.

Note: Measurements reflect the actual thickness of dimensional lumber.

Fasten the cleats between the rails to construct the panel frames.

Attach a slat at each end of the panel frame so the outer edges of the slats are flush with the outer edges of the frame.

Directions: Compost Bin

BUILD THE PANEL FRAMES. The four fence-type panels that make up the sides of this compost bin are simply cedar slats that are attached to panel frames. The panel frames for the front and back of the bin are longer than the frames for the ends of the bin. Cut the end rails (A), side rails (B) and cleats (C) to length from 2 × 2 cedar. Group pairs of matching rails with a pair of cleats. Assemble each group into a frame—the cleats should be between the rails, flush with the ends. Fasten all four panel frames together with 3" deck screws driven through the rails and into each end of each cleat **(photo A)**—drill pilot holes and countersink the screw heads slightly.

ATTACH THE PANEL SLATS. The vertical slats that are attached to the panel frames are cut from 1 × 6 cedar fence boards. They are installed with 1½" spaces between them to allow air to flow into the bin. Cut all of the slats (D). Next, lay the frames on a flat surface and

place a slat at each end of each frame. Keep the edges of these outer slats flush with the outside edges of the frame, and let the bottoms of the slats overhang the bottom frame rail by 4". Fasten the outer slats to the frames with 2" deck screws, countersunk slightly **(photo B).** When the outer slats have been fastened to all of the frames, add slats between each pair of outer slats to fill out the panels.

Insert a 1½" spacing block between the slats to set the correct gap. Be sure to keep the ends of the slats aligned. Check occasionally with a tape measure to make sure the bottoms of all the slats are 4" below the bottom of the panel frame **(photo C).**

ATTACH THE FRAMES & POSTS. The four slatted panels are joined with corner posts to make the bin. Three of the panels are attached permanently to the posts, and one of the end panels is installed with hinges and a latch so it can swing open like a gate. You can use plain 4 × 4 cedar posts for the corner posts, or, for a more decorative look, you can buy prefabricated fence posts or deck rail posts with carving or contours at the top ends. For our bin, we used cedar deck rail posts with grooves and rounded corners at the tops. Cut the posts (E) to length. If you are using plain posts, you may want to do some decorative contouring or cutting at the top of each post (or attach post caps). Start the bin-assembly process by standing a post

The inner slats should be 1½" apart, with the ends 4" below the bottom of the frame.

Stand the posts and panels upright, and fasten the panels to the posts by driving screws through the cleats.

upright on a flat worksurface. Set one of the longer slatted panels next to the post, resting on the bottoms of the slats. Hold or clamp the panel to the post, making sure the back of the panel frame is flush with one of the faces of the post. Fasten the panel to the post by driving 3" deck screws through the frame cleats and into the posts—space screws at roughly 8" intervals. Stand another post on end, and fasten the other

end of the panel frame to it, making sure the posts are aligned. Then, fasten one of the shorter panels to the adjoining face of one of the posts—the back faces of the frames should just meet in a properly formed corner **(photo D).** Fasten another post at the free end of the shorter panel; then fasten the other longer panel to the posts so it is opposite the first longer panel. This will create a U-shaped structure.

ATTACH THE GATE. The unattached shorter panel is attached at the open end of the bin with hinges to create a swinging gate for loading and unloading material. If you are planning to apply a finish to your compost bin (you may want to use some exterior wood stain to keep the cedar from turning gray), you'll find it easier to apply the finish before you hang the gate. Set the last panel between the posts at the open end of the bin, and move the sides of the bin slightly, if needed, so there is about ¼" of clearance between each end of the panel and the posts. Remove the gate, then attach a pair of 3" butt hinges to the cleat, making sure the barrels of the hinges extend past the face of the outer slats. Set the panel into the opening, and mark the location of the hinge plates onto the post. Open the hinge so it is flat, and attach it to the post **(photo E).** Attach a hook-and-eye latch to the unhinged end of the panel to hold the gate in a closed position. Make sure all hardware is rated for exterior use.

Attach the hinges to the end panel frame, then fasten to the post.

Tree Surround

Turn wasted space beneath a mature tree into a shady seating area.

CONSTRUCTION MATERIALS

Quantity	Lumber
11	2 × 4" × 8' cedar
2	1 × 6" × 8' cedar
24	1 × 4" × 8' cedar

This tree surround with built-in benches provides ample seating in your yard, while protecting the base of the tree trunk. Situated in a naturally shady area, the surround/bench creates an ideal spot to relax with a good book or spend a quiet moment alone.

The tree surround can be built in four pieces in your garage or basement, then assembled on-site to wrap around the tree. As shown, the tree surround will fit a tree trunk up to 30" in diameter. But with some basic math, it's easy to adjust the sizes of the pieces so the surround fits just about any tree in your yard.

Unlike most tree bench designs, this project is essentially freestanding and does not require you to set posts (digging holes at the base of a tree can be next to impossible in some cases). And because it is cedar, it will blend right into most landscapes.

150

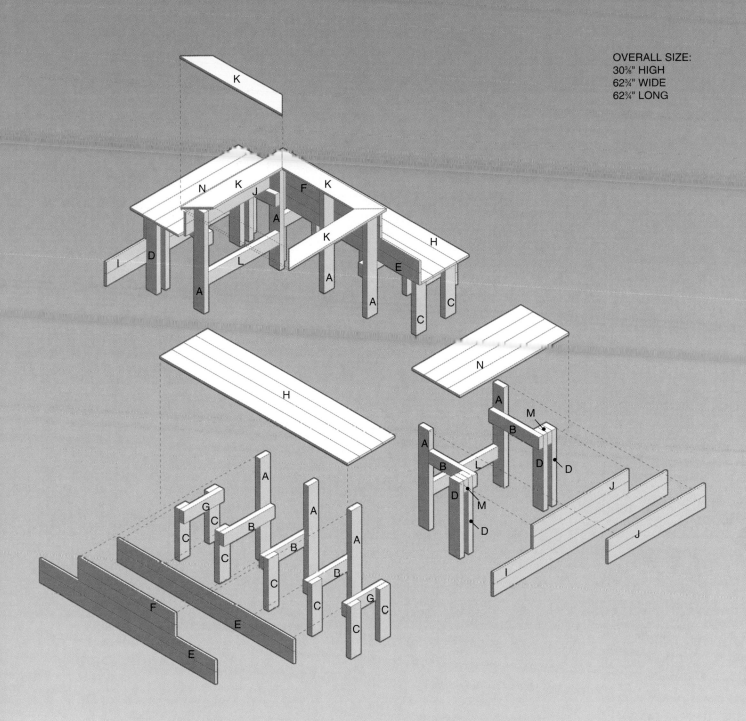

OVERALL SIZE:
30⅜" HIGH
62¾" WIDE
62¾" LONG

Cutting List

Key	Part	Dimension	Pcs.	Material
A	Inside post	1½ × 3½ × 29½"	10	Cedar
B	Seat rail	1½ × 3½ × 16¾"	10	Cedar
C	Short post	1½ × 3½ × 15"	14	Cedar
D	Long post	1½ × 3½ × 22¼"	8	Cedar
E	Face board	⅞ × 3½ × 60½"	8	Cedar
F	Face board	⅞ × 3½ × 34"	4	Cedar
G	Side seat rail	1½ × 3½ × 13¼"	4	Cedar

Cutting List

Key	Part	Dimension	Pcs.	Material
H	Bench slat	⅞ × 3½ × 62¾"	8	Cedar
I	Face board	⅞ × 3½ × 58¾"	4	Cedar
J	Face board	⅞ × 3½ × 32¼"	8	Cedar
K	End cap	⅞ × 5½ × 36"	4	Cedar
L	Stringer	1½ × 3½ × 23¼"	2	Cedar
M	Nailer	1½ × 3½ × 3½"	4	Cedar
N	Bench slat	⅞ × 3½ × 36¼"	8	Cedar

Materials: Galvanized deck screws (1½", 2½"), finishing materials.

Note: Measurements reflect the actual size of dimensional lumber.

Directions: Tree Surround

BUILD THE SHORT BENCH FRAMES. The tree surround is built as two short benches on the sides, and two taller benches on the ends. The benches are joined together to wrap around the tree. To build the support frames for the short benches, cut the inside posts (A), seat rails (B) and short posts (C) to size. Lay a short post on top of an inside post, with the bottom ends flush. Trace a reference line onto the face of the inside post, following the top of the short post. Separate the posts, and lay a seat rail across the faces of the two posts so it is flush with the outside edge and top of the short post, and just below the reference line on the inside post. Use a square to make sure the seat rails are perpendicular to the inside posts and their ends are flush with the post edges, then join the parts with moisture-resistant glue and 2½" deck screws, driven through the seat rails and into the inside posts. Drill a countersunk pilot hole for every screw used in this project. Make six of these assemblies **(photo A).** Cut the four side seat rails (G) to size. Attach them to pairs of short posts so the tops and ends are flush.

ATTACH THE SHORT BENCH FACE BOARDS. The face boards are cut in several different lengths to cover the front of each bench. Cut face boards (E) for the fronts of the short benches to length. Draw lines on the outside faces of these face boards, ⅞" and 14⅞" from each end, and at their centers. These reference lines will serve as guides when you attach the face boards to the short bench frames. Lay two frames made with two short posts on your worksurface, with the back edges of the back posts flat. Attach a face board to the top edges of the front posts, with 1½" deck screws, so the ends of the face board extend ⅞" beyond the outside edges of the frames (the seat rail should be on the inside of the frame).

TIP

Leave room for the tree to grow in trunk diameter when you build and install a tree surround. Allow at least 3" between the tree and the surround on all sides. Adjust the dimensions of your tree surround, if needed, to create additional space.

Seat rails are attached to the short posts and inside posts to make the bench frames.

The face boards attached at the tops of the short posts on the short benches should extend ⅞" past the edges of the posts.

Attach face boards to the inside posts to create the backrest. The lowest board should be ⅛" above the seat rails.

TIP

Cover the ground at the base of a tree with a layer of landscaping stone or wood bark before you install a tree surround. To prevent weeds from growing up through the groundcover, lay landscaping fabric in the area first. Add a border of landscape edging to keep everything contained. If the ground at the base of the tree is not level, you can make installation of the tree surround easier by laying a base of landscaping rock, then raking it and tamping it until it is level.

Attach another face board ⅛" below the top face board, making sure the reference lines are aligned **(photo B).**

ASSEMBLE THE SHORT BENCHES. Stand the frame and face board assemblies on their feet, then fit short bench frames made with the inside posts against the inside faces of the face boards. Center the short posts of the frames on the reference lines drawn on the face boards. Attach these frames to the face boards with 2½" deck screws. Then, set another face board at the backs of the seat rails, against the inside posts. Slip a 10d finish nail under the face board where it crosses each seat rail to create a ⅛" gap. Make sure the ends of the face board extend ⅞" beyond the edge of the frame, and attach the face board to the inside posts with 1½" deck screws **(photo C).** Attach another face board ⅛" up on the inside posts. Cut face boards (F) to fit across the inside posts with ⅞" overhang. Fasten two of these shorter face boards to each bench assembly, so the ends overhang the inside posts.

Maintain a ⅛" gap between the face boards. The top edge of the highest face board on each bench assembly should be flush with the tops of the inside posts. Cut the bench slats (H) to size. Center the bench slats on the seat rails, positioning the front bench slat first so it overhangs the face board by

1⅛" **(photo D).** Attach the front slat by driving two 1½" deck screws through each bench slat and into each seat rail. Attach the rest of the bench slats, making sure the final bench slat on each bench assembly butts against the vertical face board.

MAKE THE TALL BENCHES. The two tall benches are built almost exactly like the short benches, except they contain more face boards because of the extra height. They also have doubled posts at the front

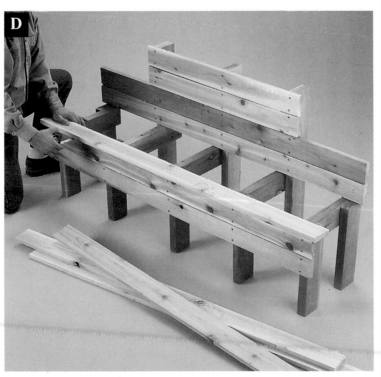

Measure to make sure the front bench slat overhangs the top face board below it by 1⅛".

for extra strength. Cut the long posts (D) and four nailers (M). Arrange the long posts in doubled pairs, with nailers in between at the tops. Fasten the doubled posts and nailers together with glue and 2½" deck screws, making sure the nailers are aligned with the fronts and tops of the posts. Then, attach a seat rail to the doubled posts **(photo E).** Attach the free end of each seat rail to an inside post, as you did for the short benches. Cut the stringers (L) to size. Position the stringers between the pairs of inside posts, at the backs of the benches, and attach them by driving 2½" deck screws through the inside posts and into the ends of the end stringers. Cut the face boards (I, J) for the tall benches. Use 1½" deck screws to attach two of the shorter boards (J) to the long posts so the top board is flush with the tops of the posts and seat rails, and the ends are flush with the outside edges of the doubled posts **(photo F).** Attach the longer face boards (I) below the shorter face boards, so they overhang the doubled posts by the same amount on each end **(photo G).** The overhang portions will cover the sides of the short benches after assembly. Attach two of the shorter face boards (J) to the front edges of the inside posts, flush with the outside edges. Cut the bench slats (N) for the tall benches. Position the slats on the seat rails, and fasten the front slat so it overhangs the front by 1⅛". Fasten a slat flush against the back of the bench, and fasten the remaining slats on each tall

After making doubled posts for the tall benches, attach the seat rails.

The shorter face boards for the tall benches are attached so the ends are flush with the outsides of the doubled posts.

bench so the spaces between slats are even.

APPLY THE FINISH. Although you are not quite finished cutting parts and you haven't assembled the tree surround yet, now is a good time to apply a

finish to the benches. Sand all the surfaces to remove rough spots and splinters, then wipe the wood clean. Apply at least two coats of exterior wood stain to protect the wood.

The longer face boards attached to the tall benches overhang the doubled posts so they cover the sides of the short benches when the tree surround is assembled.

benches fit together squarely, attach the tall benches to the short benches by driving 2½" deck screws through face boards on the tall benches and into the posts on the short benches.

ATTACH THE CAP. To give the tree surround a more finished appearance, a 1 × 6 cap with mitered corners is installed over the tops of the inside posts to make a square frame. Cut the caps (K) to full length, then draw 45° miter lines at the ends with both miters pointing inward. Make the miter cuts with a circular saw **(photo H),** or a power miter box if you have one. Attach the cap board to the bench with 1½" deck screws driven through countersunk pilot holes, then cut the three remaining cap pieces to fit, and install them. Apply the same finish to the caps that you applied to the rest of the tree surround.

ASSEMBLE THE TREE SURROUND. Carry all four benches to the tree you have built the tree surround to fit. Set the benches in a frame around the tree, so the overhang on the tall bench face boards covers the sides of the short benches. The overhanging face boards should fit flush against the recesses created by the slight overhang on the face boards on the short benches. Clamp or tack the benches together. It is likely that you will need to trim the posts on some of the frames to get the tree surround to rest so the bench seats are level. Use a carpenter's level to check the tree surround. If one side is higher than the others, set the level on the bench slats on the higher side, and tip it up until the bubble reads that it is level. Measure the distance from the level to the bench slats, then disassemble the tree surround and trim that amount from the bottoms of the posts on the higher side. Be very careful in doing this: you are always better off removing less material than you think is necessary, and trimming again if needed. Once you have trimmed the posts and reassembled the tree surround so it is roughly level, you can make minor adjustments by shimming beneath the posts with flat stones. This leveling process can be a little time-consuming, so be patient as you work. When the tree surround is level and the

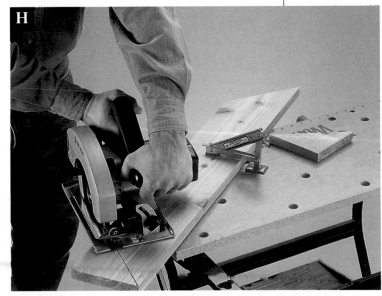

The 1 × 6 caps are mitered to make a square frame around the top of the tree surround after it is assembled around your tree.

Doghouse

Add a contemporary twist to a traditional backyard project with this cedar-trimmed, arched-entry doghouse.

CONSTRUCTION MATERIALS

Quantity	Lumber
2	1 × 2" × 8' cedar
3	2 × 2" × 8' pine
2	2 × 4" × 8' cedar
2	⅜" × 4 × 8' siding
1	¾" × 4 × 8' ABX plywood

Close your eyes and picture the first image that comes to mind when you think of a doghouse. More than likely it's a boxy, boring little structure. Now consider this updated doghouse, with its sheltered breezeway and contemporary styling. What dog wouldn't want to call this distinctive dwelling home? The sturdy 2 × 4 frame provides a stable foundation for the wall panels and roof. The main area has plenty of room to house an average-size dog comfortably, and the porch area shelters the entry, while providing an open, shady area for your pet to relax. The rounded feet keep the inside of the house dry by raising the base up off the ground.

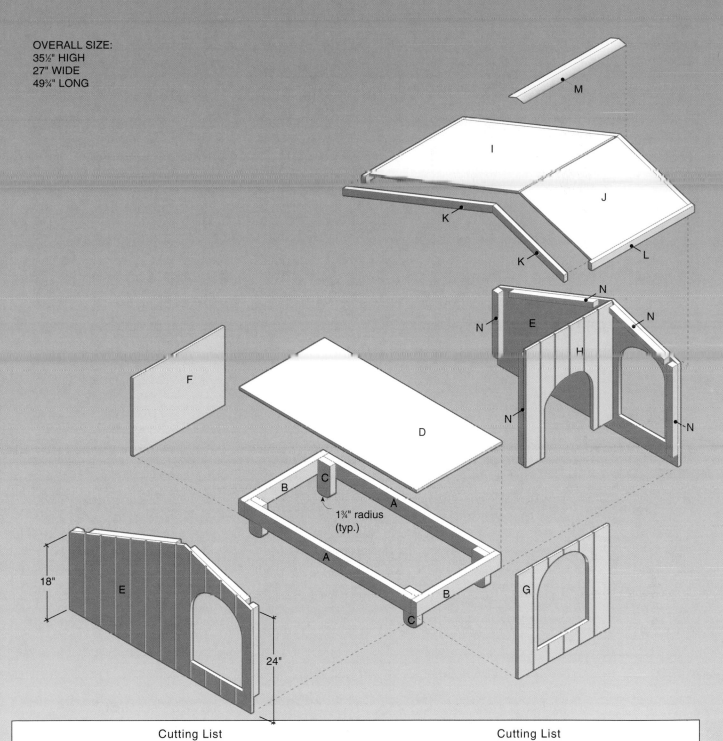

OVERALL SIZE:
35½" HIGH
27" WIDE
49¾" LONG

M

I

K

J

K

L

N

E

H

N

N

F

D

N

B

C

1¾" radius
(typ.)

A

A

B

E

18"

E

N

C

B

G

24"

Cutting List

Key	Part	Dimension	Pcs.	Material
A	Frame side	1½ × 3½ × 45"	2	Cedar
B	Frame end	1½ × 3½ × 22⅞"	2	Cedar
C	Feet	1½ × 3½ × 7½"	4	Cedar
D	Floor	¾ × 22⅞ × 48"	1	ABX Plywood
E	Side panel	⅝ × 30 × 48"	2	Siding
F	House end panel	⅝ × 18 × 24⅛"	1	Siding
G	Porch end panel	⅝ × 24 × 24⅛"	1	Siding

Cutting List

Key	Part	Dimension	Pcs.	Material
H	Center panel	⅝ × 22⅞ × 29¾"	1	Siding
I	House roof	¾ × 25½ × 35"	1	ABX Plywood
J	Porch roof	¾ × 25½ × 23"	1	ABX Plywood
K	Side roof trim	⅞ × 1½ × *	4	Cedar
L	End roof trim	⅞ × 1½ × 27"	2	Cedar
M	Flashing	1/16 × 4 × 27"	1	Galv. flashing
N	Cleat	1½ × 1½ × *"	10	Pine

Materials: Deck screws (2", 2½", 3"), 6d galvanized finish nails, silicone caulk, roofing nails with rubber washers, finishing materials.

*Cut to fit **Note:** Measurements reflect the actual size of dimensional lumber.

Fasten the 2 × 4 cedar feet to the inside frame corners with 2½" galvanized deck screws.

Lay out the roof angle on the side panels using a straightedge.

Directions: Doghouse

BUILD THE FRAME & FLOOR. The frame of the doghouse is the foundation for the floor, sides and roof. It is simply built from 2 × 4 cedar lumber. Start by cutting the frame sides (A) and frame ends (B) to length. Place the frame sides between the frame ends to form a rectangle, then fasten together with 3" deck screws. Make sure to keep the outside edges flush. Next, cut the feet (C) to length. Use a compass to lay out a 1¾"-radius roundover curve on one end of each foot, then cut with a jig saw to form the roundover. Smooth out the jig-saw cuts with a power sander. Fasten a foot in each corner of the frame with 2½" deck screws **(photo A).** Be sure to keep the top edges of the feet flush with the top edges of the frame. After the frame has been assembled, cut the floor (D) to size from ¾"-thick exterior plywood and fasten it to the top of the frame with 2" deck screws. The edges of the floor should be flush with the outside edges of the frame.

MAKE THE WALLS. The walls for the doghouse are cut from ⅝"-thick siding panels—we chose panels with grooves cut every 4" for a more decorative effect. Start by cutting the side panels (E) to the full size listed in the *Cutting List* on page 157. Then, make angled cuts that form a peak on the top of the panel to create the roof line. To make the cuts, first mark points 18" up from the bottom on one end, and 24" up from the bot-

> **TIP**
>
> *With most siding products, whether they are sheet goods or lap siding boards, there is a definite front and back face. In some cases, it is very easy to tell which face is meant to be exposed, but you always need to be careful not to confuse the two.*

tom on the other end. Then, measure in along the top edge 30" out from the end with the 18" mark, and mark a point to indicate the peak of the roof. Connect the peak mark to the marks on the ends with straight

lines to create the cutting lines **(photo B).** Lay the side panels on top of one another, fastening them with a screw or two in the waste area. Then cut both panels at the same time, using a circular saw or jig saw and straightedge cutting guide. To make the arched cutouts in the front (taller) sections of the side panels, first measure and mark points 2" and 16" in from the 24"-tall end of one panel, then draw lines from the bottom to the top of the panel, through the points. Measure up 4¼" and 15¾" from the bottom edge and draw horizontal lines to complete the square. Find the centerpoint between the sides of the square cutout outline, and measure down 7" from the top of the cutout at that point. Press down on the end of a ruler so it pivots at that point, and use the ruler and a pencil like a compass to draw a curve with a 7" radius across the top of the cutout **(photo C).** Drill a starter hole at a corner of the cutout outline, then cut the opening with a jig saw **(photo D).** Trace the cutout onto the other side panel, then make that

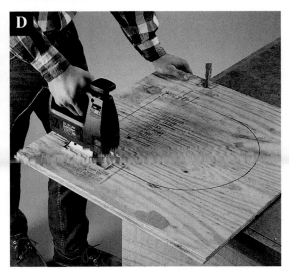

Lay out the opening archway on the side panels using a ruler and pencil.

Cut out the openings in the panels with a jig saw.

cutout. One of the side panels can also be used as a template for marking the arched cutout in the center panel and the porch end panel. First, cut the center panel (H) and porch end panel (G) to full size. Trace an arched cutout outline onto the porch end panel so the sides are 4½" from each side edge and the top is 15¾" up from the bottom. Mark an arched cutout outline on the center panel, 3⅞" from each

side edge and 15¾" up from the bottom. Make the cutouts with a jig saw, then sand all cut edges smooth.

ATTACH THE WALLS & FRAME. Cut the house end panel (F). Fasten the side panels to the frame with 2" deck screws, so the bottoms of the panels are flush with the bottoms of the frame, and the ends of the panels are flush with the frame ends. Fasten the house end panel and the porch end panel

to the frame so the bottoms of the panels are flush with the bottom of the frame (the sides of the end panels will overlap the side panels by ⅝" on each side). The 10 cleats (N) in the doghouse are used to create attaching surfaces for the roof panels and the center panel, and to tie the panel walls together. Cut them long enough to fit in the positions shown in the *Diagram* on page 157—there should be a little space between the ends of the cleats, so exact cutting is not important. Just make sure the edges are flush with the edges of the panel they are attached to. Cut the 10 cleats (N) from 2 × 2 pine, and fasten four cleats along the perimeter of each side panel, using 2" deck screws. Fasten the remaining two cleats at the edges of the back side of the center panel. Then, set the center panel between the side panels so the

TIP

If plan dimensions do not meet your needs, you can recalculate them to a different scale. The doghouse shown here is designed for an average dog (about 15" tall). If you own a larger dog, add 1" to the size of the entry cutouts and panels for every inch that your dog is taller than 15".

Fasten the center panel by driving screws through the side panels into the cleats. Use a combination square to keep the panel even.

Cut each side roof trim piece to fit between the peak and the end of the roof panel, mitering the ends so they will be perpendicular when installed. Attach all the roof trim pieces with galvanized finish nails.

front is aligned with the peak in the roof. Make sure the center panel is perpendicular, and attach it with 2" deck screws driven through the side panels and into the cleats at the edges of the center panel **(photo E)**.

ATTACH THE ROOF & TRIM. The roof and trim are the final structural elements to be fastened to the doghouse. Cut the house roof (I) and porch roof (J) to size from ¾"-thick exterior plywood. Fasten the roof panels to the cleats at the tops of the side walls, making sure the edges of the panels butt together to form the roof peak. Next, cut the trim pieces to frame the roof (K, L) from 1 × 2 cedar. The end roof trim pieces are square-cut at the ends, but the ends of the side roof trim pieces (K) need to be miter-cut to form clean joints at the peak and at the ends, where they

will meet the end trim. To mark the side trim pieces for cutting, first cut the side trim pieces so they are an inch or two longer than the space between the end of the roof panel and the roof peak. Lay each rough trim piece in position, flush with the top of the roof panel. On each trim piece, mark a vertical cutoff line that is aligned with the end of the roof panel. Then, mark a cutoff line at the peak, making sure the line is perpendicular to the peak. Cut the trim pieces with a power miter saw or miter box and

backsaw. Attach the trim pieces to the side panels with 6d galvanized finish nails **(photo F)**.

APPLY FINISHING TOUCHES. Sand all the wood surfaces smooth, paying special attention to any sharp edges, then prime and paint the doghouse. Use a good-quality exterior primer and at least two coats of paint, or you can do as we did and simply apply two or three coats of nontoxic sealant to preserve the natural wood tones. We used linseed oil. When the finish has dried thoroughly, cut a strip of galvanized steel flashing (M) to cover the roof peak (or you can use aluminum flashing if you prefer). Use tin snips or aviator snips to cut the flashing, and buff the edges with emery paper to help smooth out any sharp points. Lay the flashing lengthwise on a wood scrap, so the flashing overhangs by 2". Bend the flashing over the edge of the board to create a nice, crisp peak, then attach the flashing with roofing nails with neoprene (rubber) washers driven at 4" intervals **(photo G).**

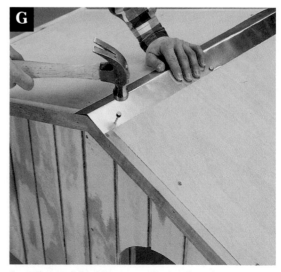

Install metal flashing over the roof peak, using roofing nails with rubber washers.